[handwritten inscription]
Due neappier
desire to see the
captives out free.
God's blessings
be upon you,
David Thomas

FROM THE HEART OF AN INTERCESSOR

Seeking His Face and Capturing His Heart

Volume 2

David L. Thomas

Anderson Publishing
Douglasville, GA

Anderson Publishing
P. O. Box 5544
Douglasville, GA 30154
www.andersonpub.com

Table of Contents

From The Heart of His Princess. . .a Tribute to Her Beloved Warrior

As you read and pray the prayers found in this book, I challenge you to find on each page a love letter from my husband to the Body of Christ. These prayers are not merely written with ink, but with the all-powerful Spirit of the living God whom David loved and served fervently and passionately with all of his heart.

God unexpectedly whispered David's name on August 23, 2000 leaving so many of us without the one we loved to have pray for us and do spiritual battle for us. I am so honored to have been the one to be by his side all those years. He was the Job 29 man personified with a raging beauty and blazing holiness. I was blessed beyond measure by his example of tenacious, prevailing, and uncompromisingly righteous prayer. My years of spiritual "boot camp" at David's side are best described with Oswald Chamber's statement: *"prayer does not equip us for greater works, PRAYER IS THE GREATER WORK."*

The lifetime of hours he spent in the Father's throne

room are recorded in Heaven. Now his life and testimony have been imparted to me and, with great resolve, I carry the mantle he left. I often hear his voice in my spirit as I pray and I hope that, as you turn the pages and read some of his mightiest prayers, you, too, will hear the voice of the one we all loved so dearly. Since the tragic events on September 11, 2001, I have asked that my two favorite prayers of his be included in this volume of prayers. They are entitled *Father Heal Our Land* and a *Prayer For Our Nation*. David knew many years earlier that America's only hope and security were for our nation to turn back to God.

It has been said that the unfinished friendships of this life suddenly become our dearest experiences and most glorious hopes. My beloved Warrior enriched my life with divine experiences that continue unto this day and will reach into eternity.

The words of Catherine of Sienna are forever etched in my testimony—"*Make two homes for thyself, my daughter. One actual home. . .and another spiritual home, which thou are to carry with thee always. . . .*" Although David died as we were building our actual new home together last year, the spiritual home he built for me was based on a firm foundation. It has not been diminished with his death but has grown and become a haven for others. Thank you, Warrior, for loving me with the heart of an intercessor, the very heart of God Himself. You are still my heartbeat and forever joined with us in the secret place of prayer.

~~*Princess*~~

FATHER HEAL OUR LAND

Dear Lord, raise up a company of worshippers in Atlanta who will lavishly praise You, and at this moment, help us to orchestrate together with a network of intercessors who can move in the awesome power of unified prayer.

Prepare our hearts, forgive our sins, cleanse us thoroughly by the blood of Jesus Christ so we can corporately pray effectual prayers which avail very, very much at this critical hour of our nation.

Lord, as our nation hangs in the balance, we are cast into the valley of decision, and time is of the essence. We pray that You would sovereignly move on Your people to take a resolute stand for righteousness, godliness, morality, and scriptural standards.

We pray that You would awaken a slumbering, complacent Church and with the stroke of Your hand, jolt us out of our apathy. Forgive us, Lord, for inhaling the deadly ether of the spirit of this age. We repent of allowing the enemy, as it states in the book of Joel, to overrun our walls and invade our homes while we were asleep. We repent on behalf of the Lord Jesus Christ in the last presidential election *[1996]*, that 40% of Christians didn't even trouble themselves enough to register to vote. Help them to realize what you say in Psalm 12:8,

**"The wicked freely strut about
when what is vile is honored among men."**

 We repent of our lethargy which has allowed the same conditions to prevail as in the day of Isaiah which produced a dearth of heroes, warriors, judges, prophets, elders, captains, men of rank, counselors and skilled craftsmen.

We repent as the Church of the Lord Jesus Christ for allowing men in government who give safe haven and support to sodomites, perverts and the slaughter of the unborn. We repent as the Church for allowing those in government who will remove the Ten Commandments and prayer from school and support and encourage fornication by the dispensing of condoms. Etch into our brains and hearts the truth of Proverbs 14:34,

**"Righteousness exalts a nation,
but sin is a disgrace to any people."**

We repent of having become a nation of discards and rejects; our consciences have become cauterized, our hearts hardened and our sensitivities have become seared. Consequently, life has become cheap. We readily, without cringing, throw away babies just as if we were dispensing of bags, bottles and boxes. God, have mercy on us. The blood of these little ones is crying out to avenge such a holocaust in this nation. Move swiftly, Lord God Almighty, while Your hand is still extended, while we still are under Your grace.

Remove the evil stench which has flowed freely in our land ever since the brilliant "politically correct" amoral think tanks of the higher courts, who call light darkness and darkness light, have opened the floodgates for immoral putrefaction and raw sewage to flow freely in our schools, streets, and living rooms. In the place of this, bring back the wind of Your Spirit which is full of the fragrance and beauty of the Lord. Let God arise and the enemy be scattered. Bring back old-fashioned holiness and purity. Return to our society leadership who by their lives, influence, example and right decisions will restore integrity, moral values, and Godly ethics to this nation.

By Your grace, we will pay the price. We will be lovers of God more than lovers of pleasure. We will turn away from a creature-comfort mentality. We choose to leave the lap of luxury and the couch of comfort, trouble ourselves, and by the grace of God, we will become spiritual vigilantes. We pray according to Isaiah 62:1,

"For Zion's sake we will not keep silent, for Jerusalem's sake we will not remain quiet, till her righteousness shines out like the dawn, her salvation like a blazing torch."

We also pray according to that same passage that we would "awake, awake, put on our strength. . .; put on our beautiful garments, . . .shake ourselves from the dust; arise, sit erect in a dignified place, . . . and loose ourselves from the bonds of our neck . . ."

We pray to raise up the righteous and put down the wicked. Raise up men and women of God who don't have price tags hanging on them, who can't be bought at any price, who are not hypnotized by the smell of money. Raise up leaders who are more concerned about the moral climate of our country than they are of being re-elected. Bring forth men and women of God who can't be leveraged, manipulated, pressured, maneuvered, or controlled.

Bring a new generation of leaders who can move against the tide, who are not swept along by the spirit of this age, who are courageous, stalwart and have the spiritual fiber and moral fortitude to stand for righteousness; who honor the Godly foundation and roots of our nation and let the chips fall where they may. We plead for leaders who will boldly proclaim in the face of the gods, and the bad breath of the adversary himself, "As for me and my house, my administration, my office, my senate chambers, my jurisdiction of authority, we will serve the Lord!"

At this strategic hour of history, we plead with You, Lord God of Israel, to raise up Elijahs and Jeremiahs who will speak with a prophetically courageous voice and call this nation back to its moorings, back to its senses, back to its sanity, back to its foundation, back to its knees, and back to its God.

Lord, our children need to witness some Daniels, who in the face of dire pressure will throw open their blinds three times a day, get on their knees, and in the sight of the Asherahs, Baals' groves, images and peer pressure, declare that God is God above all gods, King above all kings, Lord of Lords, and witness the mouth of the lion being muzzled and shut by the angel of the Lord.

Lord, our children need to witness some Shadrachs, Meshachs and Abednegos who will not bend the knee to

Baal, who will not capitulate to the pressures around them and rather will choose to be thrown into the fiery furnace, and be plucked out of the inferno without the smell of smoke by an astounded, trembling king who will freely acknowledge of a truth, Your God reigns.

Blow the trumpet in Zion; sound the alarm on Your holy hill. Give us Your grace, and a sense of urgency, we who are called by Your name to humble ourselves and pray and seek Your face, and turn from our wicked ways. Then, You will hear from heaven and will forgive our sin and will heal our land. Lord, Atlanta and America are hemorrhaging from perversion and wickedness. Our land desperately needs healing. We thank You that there is still time. Your grace is still extended over us. Your mercy is still evident. The window of opportunity is still open. Help us to buy up the time and apply our hearts to wisdom.

We ask You to raise up Godly fathers, Godly husbands, Godly councilmen, Godly mayors, governors, senators and a God-fearing president. We beseech You, Lord God Almighty, in Whom there is no shadow of turning, to raise up a Godly president, who does not have blood on His hands, to lead this nation. We place ourselves on an intercessory vigil. We move into a position of travailing prayer. We are willing to stand in the gap and make up the hedge, and be counted as one of Your prayer warriors.

We ask You, Lord, to raise up millions of green-beret prayer warrior intercessors who will storm the portals of heaven and plunder the gates of hell at one of the most crucial and pivotal times of the history of America. Rend the heavens, Lord, come down. Thank You for the promise, that when the enemy comes in like a flood, You will raise up a standard against him. We thank You also that when the enemy comes in, like a FLOOD You will raise up a standard against him.

We ask You, Lord, to bring a revival of intercessory prayer power to the extent, that once again we would be able to drive back the invading, dark hordes; put to flight the foreign alien armies of diabolical darkness; serve eviction papers on master spirits, territorial and world rulers, principalities, powers, spirit forces of wickedness, satanic highnesses and demonic nobilities. Reverse the trend. Create a vacuum of evil so righteousness can rule and reign. We thank You that according to Scripture, when God arises, there is no contest. The only thing the enemy can do is to be thoroughly scattered.

By the grace and tenacity and resilience of the living God, we are going to pray 'til You raise up the righteous and put down the wicked and righteousness rules and reigns. We are going to pray 'til the environment of this city and our neighborhoods is not conducive for evil, but becomes a wellspring of righteousness, equity and morality. By the grace of God, we are going to pray 'til You put a halt to miscarriages of justice, and there will come forth from our court systems just and equitable decisions, and if those in authority refuse this kind of judicial integrity, You would replace them so speedily with Godly men and women, that it would cause heads to turn, ears to tingle, and send shock waves of the fear of God throughout Atlanta and this nation. Let the fear of God fall upon Atlanta and America. Lord, raise up in this nation stalwart, courageous Godly leadership that will act to silence the cry of blood that arises from the ground because of the carnage of over 30 million massacred babies, some of whom are future apostles, prophets, evangelists, teachers and pastors, that will be free of strange and perverse mixtures and will not embrace Sodom and Gomorrah, and at the same time spout off Scripture out of context, who will contend for the widow and orphan and homeless, who will defend the righteous, who will have the spiritual authority to drive out from our school systems what Scripture calls demonic desert beasts, screech owls, things that mutter and peep, and creep and crawl, and bring back the basics, reading, writing, 'rithmetic and righteousness.

Help us to pray until You raise up the righteous and put down the wicked until You would cause to ascend to Capitol Hill those spoken of in Psalm 24:3, 4 who have clean hands and a pure heart, who do not lift their soul to an idol or swear by what is false, who will receive a blessing from the Lord, and vindication from God their Savior, who will be part of the generation who seeks the Lord, who diligently seek the face of their God.

Etch graphically into our brains and hearts what Your Word says in Proverbs 14:34.

**"Righteousness exalts a nation,
but sin is a disgrace to any people."**

You are our rock and our fortress, for the sake of Your name lead and guide us (Psalm 31:3). Send forth Your light and Your truth, let them guide us, let them bring us to your holy mountain, to the place where you dwell (Psalm 43:3). From the ends of the earth we call to You, we call as our heart grows faint; lead us to the rock that is higher than us

(Psalm 61:2). Lead us, Lord God, and raise up anointed, Godly leaders in this crucial hour.

Raise up the righteous, put down the wicked. Let God arise and the enemy be scattered. The victory is ours. The battle is the Lord's.

Thank You for hearing our prayer. We are greatly encouraged in the Lord this day. The effectual, fervent prayer of a righteous person avails very, very much.

In Jesus' name we pray. Amen.

PRAYER FOR OUR NATION

Dear Lord, we declare today, in the power of corporate prayer, that the ruling spirit over Marietta and Cobb County is the Holy Spirit. Open the gates for the King of Glory to come in, the Lord strong and mighty, the Lord mighty in battle. Lord, we're hungry and thirsty and desperate for You. Our soul thirsts for You, our body longs for You, in a dry and weary land where there is no water. Rend the heavens. Come down. Meet us in this time of prayer. Etch into our hearts that the effectual, fervent prayer of a righteous person avails very, very much.

Let the way of the Lord be prepared. Let every high and arrogant thing be brought low. Let every low and oppressed thing be raised up. Let the crooked ways be made straight and rough places plain so that the glory of the Lord can be ushered back into Your Church and back into this city. Lord, we want to see Your glory. We claim Your Word, that if we, Your people, who are called by Your name would humble ourselves and pray and seek Your face, and turn from our wicked ways, then You would hear from heaven and forgive our sin and heal our land. Lord, Marietta, Atlanta and America desperately need healing.

Therefore, we humble ourselves and pray and seek Your face and turn from our wicked ways. Forgive us, Lord, of all our sins. Cleanse us by the precious blood of Jesus. Protect us by that same blood as we pray.

We cannot afford the luxury of resentment and bitterness. Right now, we lay it down. We repent of being lovers of pleasure more than lovers of God. We repent for lukewarmness and having made peace with mediocrity. Let the zeal of the Lord of hosts consume us. Let the Lord Jesus Christ become our magnificent obsession.

We repent of our unanointed religious exercises in futility. We repent of quenching the spirit and extinguishing His fire. We repent of having a form of godliness, but denying the power thereof. We repent of prayerlessness. Lord, we ask You to reduce us back down to the simplicity which is in Christ Jesus, and return the Church in Marietta back to its initial mandate. If it's known for anything, it will be known as a house of prayer for all nations.

We thank You, Lord, that Your people are coming out of bondage. We've been in captivity, under a cruel taskmaster, making bricks without straw long enough. We're taking our harps down from the willow trees. We're setting our faces like flint. We're launching into the deep. We're burning our bridges behind us. We're putting our hands to the plow and we're not looking back. And, by the grace of God, we're going to dispossess the gates of the enemy, plunder the camp of darkness, and we're taking Cobb County back for the glory of God.

Lord, teach us how to pray. Raise up green-beret intercessor prayer warriors who are in their element when they pray, who know how to stand in the gap, make up the hedge, weep over a city, take hold of the horns of the altar, who won't take "no" for an answer, and will relentlessly take an assignment all the way to the gates.

Lord, we need You. Unless You do it, it's not going to happen. Unless the Lord builds the house, its builders labor in vain. Unless the Lord watches over the city, the watchmen stand guard in vain. Lord, we desperately need Your anointing this morning, that anointing which breaks the yoke, binds up the brokenhearted, brings freedom for captives, release for prisoners, comforts all who mourn, bestows on those who grieve a crown of beauty instead of ashes, the oil of gladness instead of mourning, and a garment of praise instead of a spirit of despair.

Lord, there's enough spiritual firepower in this square to shake Marietta and Atlanta to its foundation. You said when we get in agreement, one of us shall put to flight a thousand, two—ten thousand, three—a hundred thousand, four—a million, seven—a billion. Everyone of us here in unity represents the decimal moving over one more to the right. There's not a super computer in America that has enough zeros to calculate this kind of power. It's awesome!

Therefore, in this solemn assembly, in the credible exponential power of corporate prayer agreement, with the protective blood of Jesus applied to our lives, we ask You these next few moments to transform us into a loving executive body to send forth decrees into the heavenlies that will not cease nor desist until You move here on earth, in Marietta, with awesome, supernatural power. Purge and cleanse this entire area by the blood of Jesus Christ. Send angels to help and protect us. This afternoon, let our enemy know he has met more than his match. Lord, move out as a valiant, conquering warrior in great conquest as the Lord strong and mighty in battle.

Drive out demonic beasts and everything that mutters and peeps and creeps and crawls. Let principalities and powers and territorial spirits gasp and crash and burn. Let there be a major shift in the heavenlies. Help us realize today the initiative is ours and the scepter is being placed back into our hands. Bring back Your majesty, Your grandeur, Your magnificence. Bring back Your glory. Let God arise and just as the smoke flees before the wind, and just as the wax melts before the fire, let His enemies be scattered. We thank You, Lord, when God arises, it's no contest. The enemy must be scattered.

Listen up, you spirit forces of darkness. This day, in the awesome power of corporate prayer agreement, we serve eviction papers on you. You may have come this far, but you're not coming any further. The Lord rebuke you. You will no longer run roughshod over God's people as if it were open season on Christians. The day is over that Cobb County and Atlanta are known as cities of crime and perversion. In the days to come they will be internationally famous as a safe haven, cities of refuge, and places where great revival is breaking out.

We decree and declare the Lordship and superiority and supremacy of Jesus Christ over this entire area of Marietta and Cobb County. We prophesy to the north, south, east and west. Come, Holy Spirit of God. Fill this place with Your glory. Let us hear the rustling of Your garments on

Interstates 75, 85, 285 and GA 400. Bring glory back into the Church. Bring glory back into this city. Let every resident in Cobb County know there's a God in Israel, there's a God in the United States of America, and there's a God over Marietta.

We thank You, Lord, that because of revival in prayer, that we are on the threshold of a historically, unprecedented spiritual awakening. We thank You, Lord, that homosexuals and lesbians, who have been so desperate for love and affection that they have been willing to sign a death warrant just to get a little affection, that a major revival is coming to them. We thank You, Lord, that the power of God is preparing to set them free. We thank You, Lord, some of the most anointed last day ministries are going to be raised up from the ranks of repentant, radically saved homosexuals.

We thank You, Lord, that if man refuses to bring his torch into Cobb County because we refuse to embrace a perverted lifestyle, then You're going to bring Your torch into Cobb County, the Holy revival fire of God. Bring it on!

We thank You, Lord, that where sin abounds, grace does much more abound.

We thank You, Lord, that though darkness covers the earth and gross darkness the people, that in direct proportion, as we speak, the light is brightly shining upon Your people.

We thank You, Lord, that what the enemy meant for evil, You are, as we speak, turning it for good. We thank You, Lord, that when the enemy comes in like a flood, You will raise up a standard against him. We thank You, Lord, when the enemy comes in, like a FLOOD You will raise up a standard against him.

We thank You, Lord, that You're about to do a thing in Marietta and Atlanta that will cause the ears of everyone who hears of it to tingle.

We thank You, Lord, that the day is coming when the knowledge of the glory of the Lord will fill the earth as the waters cover the sea. We thank You, Lord, that the glory of the latter house will greatly exceed that of the former.

We thank You, in Jesus' name, that You have saved the best wine 'til last.

God bless Marietta. God bless Atlanta and God bless America.

Before We Pray . . .

From The Heart of an Intercessor consists of prayers gleaned from seven years of praying for the city of Atlanta every Monday morning on two Christian radio stations.

Looking back over this time, I realize it is an honor and responsibility to attempt to articulate the Father's heart for this world-class city. Jesus is our example when it comes to fervently interceding for the town where you live. He mounted the hill of Jerusalem, wept over the city, and prayed passionately with a note of desperation for that area.

"O Jerusalem, Jerusalem, you who kill the prophets and stone those sent to you, how often I have longed to gather your children together, as a hen gathers her chicks under her wings, but you were not willing. Look, your house is left to you desolate. For I tell you, you will not see me again until you say, 'Blessed is He who comes in the name of the Lord.'"
Matthew 23:37-39

There are two options for every city in America, as is made clear in this Scripture. Either our house (spiritual and family) is left desolate, sinking deeper into degradation and wickedness, or through strong prevailing prayer and fasting, we see the tide turned, principalities and powers pulled down, and the glory and awesome anointed presence of the Lord ushered back into our churches, homes and society.

One of our primary burdens during these prayers has been to challenge the modern American Church to be reduced back to the simplicity which is in Christ Jesus (2 Corinthians 11:3), and returned back to its initial mandate to be known as a "house of prayer for all nations" (Mark 11:17). This is accomplished by a "Jeremiah prayer anointing" which uproots, tears down, destroys and overthrows man's humanistic religion so the Lord can build and plant His true New Testament Church (Jeremiah 1:10).

The heart of an intercessor is graphically described in Lamentations 2:11-12. It is a picture of a fervent intervener who totally identifies with the heartbeat of the Father concerning the condition of their city.

"My eyes fail from weeping, I am in torment within, my heart is poured out on the ground because my people are destroyed, because children and infants faint in the streets of the city. They say to their mothers, 'Where is the bread and wine?' as they faint like wounded men in the streets of the city, as their lives ebb away in their mothers' arms."

What a picture of modern America!

God is presently raising up a special breed of intercessors. This is not just any generation. There is a portion of the remnant who have heard from God, consider it a critical mandate which at all costs must be carried out, do not want to compromise, and have opted to pay the price and take the high road. These are prayer warriors who have set their faces like flint, burned their bridges behind them, launched into the deep, put their hands to the plow and are not about to look back.

Realizing the present crucial hour of history, there is a note of urgency in these prayers for the Church to awaken, re-prioritize, shun that which is fleshly and religious, fervently seek the Lord in prayer, receive a fresh anointing, and pray in what we believe is going to be the greatest, unprecedented, historic spiritual awakening in the annals of history.

Special honor and thanks goes to my "Princess" wife, Lynn. During the last two years, she has been by my side every time I have prayed over the air for Atlanta. She is a powerful intercessor, and her standing with me, quietly pouring on the coals while I pray, has made more of a difference than I can put into words. One way of summing it up; "One shall put to flight a thousand, and two, ten thousand." Her faithful prayer support has resulted in an exponential increase in intercessory anointing which has impacted Atlanta.

May the mantle of intercession fall even more distinctly on you as you use these segments of prayer to intercede for your city.

**"The end of all things is near, therefore be clear minded
and self-controlled so that you can pray."
I Peter 4:7**

--David L. Thomas
(1939-2000)

Prayer
Asking Where the Wind of
God's Spirit is Blowing

Dear Lord, we thank You that You are the all sufficient One. You are well able, by few or by many is of no consequence, to do exceedingly abundantly above all that we ask or think. To You, the above and beyond God, we appeal in prayer this morning. Deliver us from perfunctory meetings, broadcasts or prayers. Give us an unction this morning to actually pray the Father's heart prayers. Let the air waves crackle these few moments with the awesome presence of the living God.

So that we can hear from You and pray purposeful, directed, focused, efficient and anointed prayers that avail much, we repent right now of unforgiveness, resentment, bitterness, holding grudges, and pride. We acknowledge there is an Atlanta cosmopolitan arrogance and for this we repent. We confess prayerlessness, carnality, and being a lover of pleasure more than a lover of God. We repent of control and manipulation which is rampant in our society and rampant in the Church of God. Forgive us, Lord, for

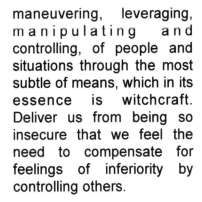

"We refuse to get involved in counterfeit religion, and close facsimiles thereof which have absolutely no life-changing essence of Your Spirit."

maneuvering, leveraging, manipulating and controlling, of people and situations through the most subtle of means, which in its essence is witchcraft. Deliver us from being so insecure that we feel the need to compensate for feelings of inferiority by controlling others.

Help us to be decisive as we release ourselves from religious exercises in futility, ecclesiastical programs which have no anointing. We refuse to get involved in counterfeit religion, and close facsimiles thereof which have absolutely no life-changing essence of Your Spirit. We thank You, Lord, that where the Spirit of the Lord is, there is liberty. We speak life to one another. Contrary to the whisperings of the evil one, you shall not die, but you shall live. Let the Lord of life and His Word of life minister to those who are listening, minister to them physically, spiritually, relationally and financially. We celebrate You as a magnanimous God of great abundance. You are a benevolent benefactor. You own the cattle on a thousand hills. We thank You, Lord, that You daily load us with benefits. Thank You, Lord, that Your mercies are new every morning. The Lord is my Shepherd, I shall not want.

For those who are hurting financially, give them the grace to begin tithing into good ground, and let them know that the heavens are bulging on their behalf, and as they repent and meet Your simple conditions, You desire to play catch-up, and restore the years, as it states in Joel 2, where the locust, cankerworm, caterpillar and palmer worm have eaten. We ask You that this week You would show them a specific token for good, and when it comes, they would know it is unmistakably from You, and that this is just the earnest money, and the rest is soon coming. Thank You we are living in days of restoration. Hasten the day, as Scripture has prophesied, when there will be large blocks of finances transferred from the wicked to the righteous for the purpose of establishing Your covenant and propagation of the Gospel. We thank You, Lord, that there's evidence that it has already begun.

We relinquish all control to You. Give us the grace of yielding, and instead of being driven to manipulate, teach us how to humble ourselves and be led by Your Spirit, and to fervently pray, and let You, Lord, bring it about Your way and in Your time. We pray that every man listening would be up-to-date with his God, and up-to-date with his wife, and keep short accounts so that his prayers will not be hindered. We pray that instead of husbands and wives trying to change each other, they would take hands off, pray diligently, and witness You going to the basement of their lives and bring about radical, pivotal changes of personality and lifestyle. Lord, You promised that those who called upon You would be delivered. Let not demon spirits be the spoiler in our lives or homes. Rid them from our marriages, from our children, from our finances. Reverse the curses, including generational ones, and bring such a radical metamorphosis in our lives, and deal so resolutely with spirits of deprivation, that we would begin to tear down our barns and build bigger just to contain the inordinate blessings of the Lord.

For those who have been languishing for years under strong rejection, self-rejection, and spirits of rejection, we ask You to give them the grace to forgive themselves, and to

3

forgive their perpetrators and accusers that brought on the rejection when they were young, and if necessary, to forgive You if they have ought against You. Etch it deeply into their minds and spirits that they are greatly accepted in the Beloved. They are Your Divine appointment on earth. No one else has the unique characteristics and qualities they have to accomplish that for which You have called them. Help them to perceive themselves as You see them, not as others cruelly speak of them. Show them the truth about themselves. Let them know they are people of destiny, that You have a specific purpose and calling upon their lives. We take authority over spirits of rejection, self-rejection, inferiority, low self-esteem and low self-image. How dare you vex the child of the living God! We serve eviction papers on you right now. For this very purpose, the Lord Jesus Christ died and shed His Blood. He came to set the captives free.

We thank You for Your purpose on this earth, Lord, that is summed up in Acts 10:38.

". . .God anointed Jesus of Nazareth with the Holy Spirit and power, and. . .He went around doing good and healing all who were under the power of the devil."

Let God arise and let the enemy be scattered. We thank You, Lord, when we let God arise, it's no contest. The only thing the enemy can do is be scattered. Let these dear people know they are the apple of Your eye, they are accepted in the Beloved, they are members of a royal nation and holy priesthood, and that You promised never to leave them nor forsake them. Thank You, Lord, for being such a great Savior, and Redeemer, Baptizer, Healer and Deliverer. We are going to bask in Your presence and rejoice in You all day long. The joy of the Lord is our strength.

Everything we do or accomplish hinges directly on answered prayer. Therefore, search our hearts, see if there is any wicked way which would short-circuit our endeavors this day. We don't want to go around in circles like the children of Israel did. We don't want to waste precious time. As the psalmist cried out in Psalm 51:10-12,

"Create in me a pure heart, O God, and renew a steadfast spirit within me.

Do not cast me from your presence or take your Holy Spirit from me.

Restore to me the joy of your salvation and grant me a willing spirit, to sustain me."

We ask You, this morning, where is the wind of Your Spirit blowing? Your Word says that "The wind blows wherever it pleases. You hear its sound, but you cannot tell where it comes from or where it is going. So it is with everyone born of the Spirit." We acknowledge, Lord, that You are a God of great order. The planets do not collide with each other overnight. Likewise, You're a God of great spontaneity. We ask You, Lord, this morning, to bring back into our lives and homes and the Church in this city, Divine order and Godly spontaneity. Remove the rubbish and clutter in our lives and minds. Deliver us from being packrats

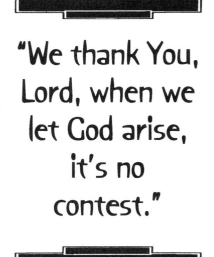

"We thank You, Lord, when we let God arise, it's no contest."

5

because of fear or lack or poverty. Trim away from us everything that was not originally birthed of Your Spirit. We thank You that whatever is born of God overcomes the world.

We wait upon You. Again, we ask You, Lord, Where is the wind of Your Spirit blowing? What are You saying this week? What is on Your agenda? What are You about to do? What season of the Lord are we in? What's going to happen in this nation? What are You about to do with the American Church? God forbid that it would be said of us that which was said of those in Jerusalem, as You wept over that city, that they did not recognize the day of Your visitation, and consequently, their cities were ravaged and plundered. We thank You that Your Word says that You do nothing except You reveal it to Your servants, the prophets. We wait upon You. We ask You, Lord, to give us revelation knowledge that will supersede anything we have ever known. We are reminded of Elisha's servant who was terrified as he looked at the circumstances, and saw a huge, threatening, overwhelming army, and as Elisha prayed for him, You Lord, opened the servant's eyes to see an even much greater angelic army preparing to swoop down on the military army. Lord, give us spiritual eyes to see and ears to hear, more than just what we see and hear with our physical eyes and ears.

We pray Paul's prayer for the Ephesian Church in Ephesians 1:17, 18.

"I keep asking that the God of our Lord Jesus Christ, the glorious Father, may give you the Spirit of wisdom and revelation, so that you may know him better.

I pray also that the eyes of your heart may be enlightened in order that you may know the hope to which he has called you, the riches of his glorious inheritance in the saints."

We humbly confess to You, Lord, we desperately need wisdom from on high. We would make a shambles of our lives if we depended, like the humanists do, just on our own human intelligence, and we pray into the lives of those listening, supernatural enlightenment. We appropriate Proverbs 3:5, 6.

"Trust in the Lord with all your heart and lean not on your own understanding;

in all your ways acknowledge him, and he will make your paths straight."

Let it be that as we are walking along, it will happen to us as is stated in Isaiah 30:21,

"Whether you turn to the right or to the left, your ears will hear a voice behind you, saying, 'This is the way; walk in it.'"

We thank You, Lord, for Your Word in Isaiah 9:6, that You are the Mighty God, Everlasting Father, Prince of Peace, but the very first attribute mentioned in this passage is, You are called Wonderful Counselor. We invite the Wonderful Counselor to fully invade every area of our lives. Remove the confusion. Remove all the Job's friends with all of their interpretations of what they think we should do. We're not interested in the ideas of flesh. Remove the smoke screens. Remove the vagueness. Remove the cycles of walking around in the dark, not having a clue as to what we should do. We ask You, Lord, to come four square upon the listeners today. Baptize them afresh and anew in Your Holy Spirit and let there come forth a quickening, a sharpness, an understanding, a supernatural knowledge, a sense of being led by Your Spirit. Your Word says that in the last days, the Spirit speaks expressly. We ask You, Lord, not only for clear direction, but let it be that out of the mouth of two or three witnesses, let everything be confirmed.

7

In Jesus' name, amen.

Additional Scripture Reference

Jeremiah 29:11-14

~2~

Prayer for
Adoration and Worship
for Who God is

Lord, it is an amazing, awesome privilege to approach Your throne room this morning and orchestrate our prayers with intercessors all over this city. The veil has been rent in twain. We no longer have to offer animal sacrifices or go through a human mediator. We come boldly before the throne of grace this morning, boldly and with confidence, to obtain mercy and find grace to help in time of need. Jesus is our Mediator.

We honor You, do homage, give obeisance to You this day. You are a great God. There is no other God like You. Give us a heart of gratitude and praise and worship this day. Cause to flow in us and through us the river which makes glad the city of God. When the sun sets, let this day go down in our diary as one in which we were preoccupied with honoring, glorifying and worshipping You.

Regardless of what happens, we will praise You. Even as Paul and Silas found themselves in great distress, in the direst of circumstances, bound with fetters and in stocks, yet at the midnight hour they praised You. So, we will praise You. Let our adoration to You ascend this morning like sweet fragrance and incense.

Remove the anger, the bitterness, the anxiety, the murmuring and complaining. Fill our hearts with thankfulness, worship and adoration to You. In our midnight hour, in the midst of our prison, right now, we resolve, with an act of our will, to pray and praise You. We issue forth prayers of worship this morning. Let the saints be swept up in praise and adoration this day. Let God arise and let the enemy be scattered.

We celebrate You as our Abba Father. We kneel before You, Father, from Whom Your whole family on earth derives its name. You are the Abiding One. If we abide in You, and You abide in us, we shall ask what we will and it shall be done. You are able. You are abounding and abundant, able to do abundantly above all that we ask, think, or imagine. You are our adequacy and sufficiency. Your grace is sufficient. You are our Adonai. You are our all, our all in all. You are able to make all grace abound to us, so that in all things, at all times, having all that we need, we will abound in every good work.

> "In our midnight hour, in the midst of our prison, right now, we resolve, with an act of our will, to pray and praise You."

We praise You as the all-knowing, the omniscient One. Nothing escapes Your eyes. You know all things. You are all-powerful. We are Your people, Your inheritance You brought out by Your great power and Your outstretched arm. Thine is the kingdom, the power and the glory, forever. You are the Almighty God. We abide under the shadow of the Almighty. You are the Alpha and the Omega, the One Who is, and Who was, and Who is to come, the Almighty. We can trust You because You know the beginning from the end. You birthed us and You have already written the last chapter.

We worship You Who are the Amen, for no matter how many promises You have made, they are yes in Christ and so through You the Amen is spoken by us to the glory of God. Let there resonate from us, internally, all day long, an amen that orchestrates with Your Amen.

You are the anointed of God. Your anointing breaks the yoke, binds up the brokenhearted, proclaims freedom for the captives, release for the prisoners, comforts those who mourn, provides for those who grieve, bestows on us a crown of beauty instead of ashes, the oil of gladness instead of mourning, a garment of praise instead of a spirit of despair.

You are the Answer. Since the answer arises in us, help us to be ready to give an answer to every one who asks of us the reason of our hope. You are the Architect and Builder. We, like Abraham, look forward to the city with foundations, whose architect and builder is God. You are the Ascended One. When You ascended on high, You led captives in Your train; You received gifts from men.

Thank You, Lord, You are our Atonement—the eternal sacrifice for all our sins. This day, regardless of how we feel, we stand in Christ's righteousness.

You are the Author and Finisher of our faith. Help us to

11

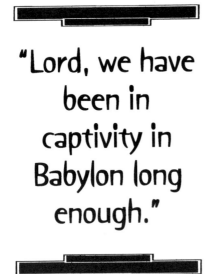

"Lord, we have been in captivity in Babylon long enough."

throw off everything that hinders and the sin that so easily entangles, and let us run with perseverance the race marked out for us. Let us fix our eyes on You, Jesus, the Author and Perfecter of our faith.

You are our Authority and just as You commissioned the twelve disciples with Your authority, so You vest it in us—power and authority to drive out demons, to cure diseases, to preach the kingdom of God, and to heal the sick.

You are Available, ever ready for us to have instant access to the throne of God.

You are our Avenger. We release all plans we have to get even or for retribution, for vengeance is Yours, You will repay.

You are Awesome. We stretch expletives and strain superlatives to try to explain how awesome You are. We could not begin to articulate the breadth and width and height and depth and scope and magnitude of Your awesomeness. Our God is an Awesome God.

You are the Balm of Gilead. When Your people are crushed, there is a Balm in Gilead. There is a great Physician. There is healing for the wounds of Your people.

Thank You, Lord, that You are Beautiful. In a world that has been corrupted, perverted, distorted, contaminated and putrefied, what a contrast to your magnificent beauty. Splendor and beauty are before You, strength and glory are in Your sanctuary. You are before all things and in You all things are held together and consist.

Lord, we have been in captivity in Babylon long enough. Our harps have hung on the poplar trees. As long as our harps have hung, so our heads have hung. Our captors and tormentors demanded of us songs of joy. They said, "Sing us one of the songs of Zion!" How can we sing the songs of the Lord while in a foreign land?

But now, as we are released from captivity in Babylon, once again, we take our harps down from the trees where they have hung, where our heads were bowed down, and once again we sing the songs of Zion unto You and as we worship You in prayer and in song, You are the lifter of our heads. Give unto the Lord, all ye mighty, give unto the Lord glory and strength. Give unto the Lord the glory due His name. For You are worthy to be praised this day. What an honor!

In Jesus' name, amen.

Additional Scripture Reference

Psalm 47:1-9

~3~

Prayer for
the Sovereignty of God

This morning we desire to do kingdom business with You. We thank You for Your promise that if we call unto You, You would answer us and show us great and unsearchable things we do not know. We thank You, Lord, that when we cry to You that You answer us from Your Holy Hill (Psalm 3:4).

Psalm 9:10
"Those who know your name will trust in you, for you, Lord, have never forsaken those who seek you."

Let these few moments of prayer be decisive, be life-changing and life-redirecting for many who are listening. Let the deck be cleared, let the way of the Lord be prepared so that every word will be highly efficient in the realm of the Spirit, hit its target, and in a matter of a few minutes or a few days or a few weeks or months, according to Your Divine timetable, these prayers, prayed will bear fruit. Then it will be confirmed to those listening, that indeed, the effectual, fervent prayer of a righteous person avails very, very much. Then everyone will know that there is a God in Israel, there is a God over the United States of America, and there is a God over Atlanta.

With an act of our own volition, right now, we repent and close every door of access to the adversary to harass, vex, or frustrate Your people. We claim the Scripture in Hebrews 12:15, *"See to it that no one misses the grace of God and that no bitter root grows up to cause trouble and defile many."*

We confess every unforgiveness, resentment, grudge, desire for revenge and bitterness. God forbid that any root of bitterness would grow in us, cause trouble and defile not only us, but those around us.

For those who are a little shaky this morning, who are uncertain about their future, they're traveling uncharted waters, they're facing difficult circumstances, help them to know this day, as they trust You with all their heart, and rely not on their own resources or understanding, that indeed You are a Sovereign God, and You have everything under control. We pray that You will help stabilize them and be an anchor to their soul.

We thank You, Lord, You are such a Sovereign God, You know the end from the beginning, that You, according to Psalm 33:10, foil the plans of the heathen, You thwart the purposes of evil people, and Your plans stand firm forever and the purposes of Your heart throughout all generations. You foil the signs of false prophets and make fools of diviners. You overthrow the learning of the wise and turn it into nonsense. You carry out the words of Your servants and fulfill the predictions of Your messengers. Encourage Your people this day that You are a Sovereign God, and that indeed, You do have everything under control.

This morning, we celebrate You as all sovereign, all powerful God. All authority and might are Yours. You are the

Alpha and the Omega—the beginning and the end, and consequently, You know the beginning from the end. Nothing takes You by surprise. As is stated in Psalm 119:91, *"Your laws endure to this day, for all things serve you."* We thank You, Lord, that You are so redemptive, that all circumstances can end up

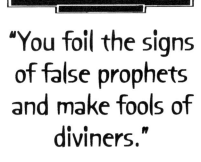

"You foil the signs of false prophets and make fools of diviners."

being Your servants. You even use sin and darkness to cause people to become desperate, until the evil one overplays his hand, they get thoroughly tired of what the enemy has to offer, and they come to realize that the kicks have their kickbacks, and that sin has a payday—the wages of sin are death and that whatever the evil one offers has a law of diminishing returns.

We thank You, Lord, that in Your sovereignty, regardless of how things appear on the surface now, that as we seek You, Your Word says in Philippians 1:6, *being confident of this, that he who began a good work in you will carry it on to completion until the day of Christ Jesus."*

Thank You, Lord, that You specialize in turning the tables on darkness, and even as You hardened Pharaoh's heart, and at that moment, it appeared as if everything was going backwards, and appeared that the enemy had the upper hand, You were doing this to set an ambush for darkness, achieve great victory for Your children, and get glory to Yourself. We thank You, Lord, in Your sovereignty, that what the adversary meant for evil, as Your people pray, You historically have turned it into good. Thank You, Lord, that where sin abounds,

17

grace does all that much more abound. Thank You, Lord, based on Psalm 92:7, *"that though the wicked spring up like grass and all evildoers flourish, they will be forever destroyed."* Thank You, Lord, that even though darkness covers the earth and thick darkness the people, the light is arising upon Your Church. Give us Your perspective, Your outlook. Give us the mind of Christ to see things as You see them—the way they really are.

Help Your people to know that when they have done everything they know to do—humble themselves, pray, seek Your face, turn from their wicked ways, be obedient, sensitive to Your Spirit, up-to-date with their forgiveness and tithing—that regardless of the circumstances or the way things appear, You indeed are a Sovereign God and You have the last Word.

Lord, we acknowledge Your sovereignty over all things, including everything in our lives—spouses, children, home, jobs, business, finances, ministry. You are Lord over all. Thank You, Lord, for Your sovereignty and hearing our prayer. In Jesus' name, amen.

Additional Scripture Reference

1 Chronicles 29:11-12

~4~

Prayer for Wisdom

Dear Lord, this morning we humbly acknowledge that aside from Your wisdom, we know nothing, and apart from Your guidance and leadership, we would surely go astray. Unless we hear a word from the Lord, "This is the way, walk ye in it," our ship will surely end up on the rocks.

We celebrate the fact that in Your sovereign purposes You have made foolish the wisdom of this world. The foolishness of God is wiser than man's wisdom, and the weakness of God is stronger than man's strength.

We approach Your throne this morning. We must have a word from the Lord! There are some out there that are waiting upon You. They cannot take another step until they unmistakably hear and have confirmed a word from You! Time is of the essence. We have bankrupted our own way. We have run out of intellectual options. We have expended our energies frantically searching for truth at secular cesspools. All we like sheep have gone astray. Each of us has turned to his own way. The think tanks of this world, relying upon their own brilliance and genius have shipwrecked and left a path of strewn wreckage of intellectual disaster.

"To the man who pleases him, God gives wisdom, knowledge and happiness, but to the sinner he gives the task of gathering and storing up wealth to hand it over to the one who pleases God. This too is meaningless, a chasing after the wind.

Ecclesiastes 2:26

This morning, with decisiveness, we flee the ash heap of fleshly humanism contriving in its own genius a fast-lane to self-destruction. There is a way which seems right unto a man, but the end thereof is the way of death. We need and desire and must hear a word from the Lord.

Forgive us for allowing the world system to desensitize us to the voice of Your Holy Spirit. Forgive us for our indifference, callousness, hard-heartedness, half-heartedness, apathy, complacency. Forgive us for permitting the spirit of this age to subtly cause us to lapse into a spiritual malaise. We refuse any longer to be mesmerized or leveraged by the subtle contrivances and influences of society that are cunningly engineered to get us to do things impulsively, without waiting on the Lord.

> "This morning, with decisiveness, we flee the ash heap of fleshly humanism, contriving in its own genius a fast-lane to self-destruction."

Remove from us the anesthesia of the spirit of this world. Once again, we desire with all of our hearts, Lord, to tune out the raucous, shrill, caustic, nerve-shattering, alluring siren songs of this world system, to quiet the prince and power of the air, and we desire with all of our hearts to be tuned in to Your Spirit, and once again, to discern and hear that still small voice that spoke this universe into existence.

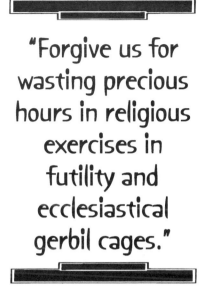

"Forgive us for wasting precious hours in religious exercises in futility and ecclesiastical gerbil cages."

Give us Your grace, Lord. Help us to rise up out of this generational stupor and find our way back to Your wisdom, Your knowledge, Your revelation, Your understanding, Your insight, Your perspective, Your vision for our lives. Forgive us for sitting at the feet of intellectual ignoramuses who feed their own egos by arrogantly pontificating their humanistic ideas and anti-Christ precepts. We have drunk at the fountain and cesspool of folly too long. We flee these bankrupt brains. Help us to buy up the years where the locust, cankerworm, palmer worm and caterpillar have eaten. Help us to buy up the time, number our days, and give ourselves to Your wisdom.

Forgive us for wasting precious hours in religious exercises in futility and ecclesiastical gerbil cages. Give us spiritual efficiency. As Paul said, we are not like those who strike out at the wind. Let every blow hit its target. Though our sins are as scarlet, they shall be white as snow. We desire to drink freely at the fountain of living waters that are crystal clear, uncontaminated, unpolluted, refreshing, invigorating, resuscitating, renewing, energizing, cleansing and so holy.

By Your strength and grace, we will shake ourselves, clothe

ourselves with Your strength, put on Your garments of splendor, shake off the dust, rise up and sit enthroned in heavenly places (Isaiah 52:2).

Speak to us, Lord. Your servants are listening. We desire for You to thoroughly change our lifestyles, our attitudes, our direction, our concepts, our perspective, our mentality. Clear out the cobwebs of flesh and carnality. Give us a renewed mindset. Give us the mind of Christ. Let the thoughts that flow directly from Your throne so flood our minds that we can say as David said, "Your thoughts are so numerous I cannot number them nor put them in order."

From here on out, however many days we have, we resolve by the grace of God, to feed on Your Word. Let the Word of Christ dwell in us richly. Let faith rise up in our hearts. You have given us the measure of faith. Hone our discernment to scorn empty religion, to pick up on subtly close religious counterfeits and deeply appreciate the things of the Spirit of God. Let us say like Job, as we go through the storms of life, I consider Your Word more vital than the food that I eat.

The same Spirit of the Lord that rested on Jesus, the Spirit of wisdom and of understanding, the Spirit of counsel and of power, the Spirit of knowledge and of the fear of the Lord, let it rest on us. This is all we want. We need no other wisdom. Just as You, Jesus, grew and became strong, and were filled with wisdom and the grace of God was upon You, so let it be said about us. In You, Lord, are hidden all the treasures of wisdom and knowledge.

"How many are your works, O Lord! In wisdom you made them all; the earth is full of your creatures."

Psalm 104:24

"By wisdom the Lord laid the earth's foundations, by understanding he set the heavens in place;"

Proverbs 3:19

". . .Praise be to the name of God for ever and ever; wisdom and power are his."

Daniel 2:20

"Oh, the depth of the riches of the wisdom and knowledge of God! How unsearchable his judgments, and his paths beyond tracing out!"

Romans 11:33

We set our faces like flint to worship and adore You all day long. You are our Savior, Lord, Master, King, Commander-in-Chief. We have no other Master. Blessed be the name of the Lord.

Thank You, Lord, for hearing our prayer this day.

In Jesus' name, amen.

Additional Scripture References

Jeremiah 10:1-3
Hear what the Lord says to you, O house of Israel. This is what the Lord says: "Do not learn the ways of the nations or be terrified by signs in the sky, though the nations are terrified by them. For the customs of the peoples are worthless; . . .

Jeremiah 10:6-8

No one is like you, O Lord; you are great, and your name is mighty in power. Who should not revere you, O King of the nations? This is your due. Among all the wise men of the nations and in all their kingdoms, there is no one like you. They are all senseless and foolish; they are taught by worthless wooden idols.

Jeremiah 10:11, 12

"Tell them this: 'These gods, who did not make the heavens and the earth, will perish from the earth and from under the heavens.'" But God made the earth by his power; he founded the world by his wisdom and stretched out the heavens by his understanding.

I Corinthians 1:18-25

For the message of the cross is foolishness to them who are perishing, but to us who are being saved it is the power of God. For it is written: "I will destroy the wisdom of the wise; the intelligence of the intelligent I will frustrate." Where is the wise man? Where is the scholar? Where is the philosopher of this age? Has not God made foolish the wisdom of the world? For since in the wisdom of God the world through its wisdom did not know him, God was pleased through the foolishness of what was preached to save those who believe. Jews demand miraculous signs and Greeks look for wisdom, but we preach Christ crucified: a stumbling block to Jews and foolishness to Gentiles, but to those whom God has called, both Jews and Greeks, Christ the power of God and the wisdom of God. For the foolishness of God is wiser than man's wisdom, and the weakness of God is stronger than man's strength.

~5~

Prayer for the Release of God's Blessings to His People

Dear Lord, we intervene and stand in the gap for thousands of frustrated Christians who read about Your blessings in the Word, but who have not personally experienced them. They are discouraged, disappointed, and some are disillusioned concerning the Christian walk and in a state of deep depression. These few short moments, Lord, meet with us. Let there be a quickening of Your Word. All of a sudden, move past all the religion these people have been involved in. Let them hear a rhema, personal word from the Lord which will arrest them and be life-changing.

Come, Lord Jesus, rend the heavens. Come down this morning. Meet Your people right where they are. You said in Psalm 102:17 that You would respond to the prayer of the destitute; You would not despise their plea. We ask You, Lord, through the indescribable power of corporate prayer, heal those who feel destitute. Set something into motion today in the lives of Your needy people which will rescue them from the pit of despair, hopelessness, deprivation, lack and want, and lift them to a new place, personally, spiritually and

25

financially. Let them know of a surety, that as they test You, as it says in Malachi 3:10, and tithe in good ground, not just religious ground, that they would personally see if You will not throw open the floodgates of heaven and pour out so much blessing that they will not have room enough for it. They would actually have to take time to tear down their barns and build bigger just to contain the blessings of the Lord, and for the first time in their lives, they would lend and not borrow. They would have a new set of prayer requests—what do we do with the overflow?

We ask You, Lord, right now to dispatch militant angels to intercept the evil one who has come to steal, kill and destroy. You foul serpentine, python spirit, which specializes in systematically choking the life out of its victims, including finances, how dare you touch God's anointed. You spirits of deprivation, lack, poverty and want, how dare you bring a reproach on God's choice vessels. How dare you make them a laughingstock and a byword to be scorned and mocked. In the power of corporate prayer, we bind you, render you null and void, break your evil throttle hold, and take authority over you to remove your filthy fangs, extract your evil venom and free God's people.

In the place of this, Lord, we ask You to release blessings, abundance, prosperity. Let Your people personally experience what You told Joshua, that as they meditate in Your Word day and night, You would cause them to prosper and have good success.

We thank You, again, that You sent Your Holy Spirit so that we would not be orphans. Remove orphanhood from Your people. Lord, let Your people rise up, as it says in Isaiah 52:2 and shake off their dust; rise up, sit enthroned, free themselves from the chains on their neck and let them know, personally, what it means when the Scripture states that where the Spirit of the Lord is, there is liberty. This includes liberty from financial bondage.

We break curses, including generational ones, remove dark spirits like that evil python, and open the floodgates of heaven, and let them come cascading down to them just like the Niagara waterfalls. Let Your people be found in such a place of obedience, walking intimately with You, hearing from You, free from the darkness of this world system, in agreement, in unity, that You would command a blessing upon them in every domain of their life, wherever they go.

> **"Lord, make these people who, heretofore, have felt like beggars and orphans, become the jealousy of this world system. . ."**

Lord, make these people who, heretofore, have felt like beggars and orphans, become the jealousy of this world system and the world would come to them and ask them of the reason of the hope within them. Lord, this is true evangelism, not just when we seek out people to witness, but when they witness our lifestyle, and the blessings of the Lord, and they seek us out. Make them curious. Make them jealous for Who and what we have.

We ask You, Lord, to re-program Your people that even though they may have been brought up under the curse of poverty, that Your inheritance for them is better. All of a sudden, give them a whole new mindset. Remove the thought system which is not of faith. Remove the mentality which they have been conditioned with over the years which is beggarly, miserly, just barely making it. Give them Your mentality, the mind of Christ. Cause to rise up inside of them a joyful

27

expectation of the good things You have for them. Help them to anticipate the good things of God, not to continually expect bad things to happen to them. Help them to order their conversation and lifestyle in such a manner, that they will speak faith, live faith, expect in faith and be provided for in faith. Help them, this day, to take the high road. Remove from their lives grumbling, complaining, murmuring, and spare them from false friends and naysayers who surround them with doubt. Network them with covenant, remnant people who can stand with them, edify them, support them in the Lord, and cause their faith to rise to new heights.

Come, Lord Jesus. This is the day of the latter rain; this is the day of restoration that the prophets of old spoke of; this is the day spoken of in Joel when You would pour out Your Spirit upon all flesh; this is the day You said You would restore the years where evil insects have eaten and robbed from Your people. This is the year in which we are celebrating Jubilee— a special time in which all of our debts are cancelled and the prisoners are released from their grueling captivity, from under a cruel taskmaster, making bricks without straw. This is the day in which we are entering into in which the glory of the latter house will greatly exceed that of the former.

Come, Lord Jesus, do a marvelous thing. Show Yourself strong on behalf of Your people. As David asked, show me a token for good, Lord, show them, this week, a token for good. When it comes, in whatever form You see fit for it to come, let them know without a doubt, this is the hand of God. This is just the earnest or down payment and the rest is shortly to follow. Lord, help us to walk humbly before You, always having a heart full of gratitude. In Jesus' name, amen.

~6~

Prayer for the Restoration of Balance and Integrity to the Body of Christ

Dear Lord, thank You this day that we can be up-to-date with You. We don't have to operate under a cloud of foreboding darkness with unsettled issues. Thank You for Your willingness at all times to forgive us. We celebrate You this day as a great Redeemer. We confess to You all of our shortcomings, all of our ulterior motives, all of our hidden agendas, all of our bitterness and anger.

Help us, Lord, to be real people. Forgive us of all our sins and cleanse us by the Blood of Jesus. We pray that these few moments of prayer agreement will be so real that someone who has been grappling with self-condemnation, who has entertained a constant barrage of negative thoughts about themselves and their abilities and their future will be released from it, right now, by the delivering power of the Spirit of the living God.

Thank You, Lord, You came to set the captives free. Thank You, Lord, that You are the very antithesis of bondage, that where the Spirit of the Lord is, there is liberty. Bring an anointing these few moments to release prisoners. Let them hear the chains drop to the ground and leave their prison cell a new person in Christ Jesus.

We pray this morning to restore balance and integrity into the Body of Christ. We pray that the Church will no longer be anemic, nor powerless, nor a laughingstock, nor resemble the Seven Sons of Sceva who mouthed words, but lacked the spiritual authority to back up the words, and in their confrontation with the adversary, ran out of the house severely beaten. Restore Your Church, Lord Jesus, to the extent that we would operate in such wisdom that even our enemies would not be able to withstand nor gainsay, and they would be forced to respect us. Help us to realize that *this* is a special year. The initiative is ours, the ball is in our court. We act and darkness must react. Let this be the year of Jubilee where captives are released and debts are forgiven.

"Lord, we not only want to know Your acts, we want to know You, personally, intimately, and unlearn the ways of religion which is riddled through and through with flesh and the carnal Babylonish strategies of this world system."

Lord, instruct us in Your ways and Your methods. Your Word says that the children of Israel knew Your acts, and Moses knew Your ways. Lord, we not only want to know Your acts, we want to know You, personally, intimately, and unlearn the ways of religion which is riddled through and through with flesh and the carnal Babylonish strategies of this world system. Reduce us back down to the simplicity which is in Christ

Jesus. Like Samuel, let none of our words drop to the ground.

We thank You for the balance in Your Word, of warfare and love, as spoken of in Psalm 144:1, 2.

"Praise be to the Lord, my Rock, who trains my hands for war, my fingers for battle. He is my loving God. . . ."

Thank You for the balance of the Scripture in Proverbs 24 of wisdom and power and knowledge and strength.

In the midst of all the eccentricities and strangeness and weirdness which has infiltrated the Body of Christ, bring back the New Testament integrity and balance. We acknowledge You this day as the Lion of Judah and the Lamb of God. We pray this balance into our lives that we would be so much under the control of Your Holy Spirit that we would know when and how to be like a tender, submissive, quiet lamb, and also know by Your Spirit when to be transformed into a militant, fierce lion, to identify with the righteous indignation of God and resist the powers of darkness. We especially pray that men in the Church will be so free from compulsive enslaving, driving spirits and raging beasts and that they will know when to be like a lion, and when to be like a lamb.

We acknowledge, Lord, that in Scriptures, Your Church is compared to a building, It's compared to a bride, and It's compared to an army. We understand the Church being like a building, we've been inside plenty of buildings. We understand the Church being like a bride, we've been to many weddings. Lord, the Church in Atlanta and America doesn't understand true spiritual warfare because we've never had tanks and troops marching up and down our streets. Just like when apostle Paul observed a gaping hole or obvious deficiency in the Church, he didn't criticize nor condemn, he

"Lord, teach us. . .to war a good warfare."

prayed to fill up that which was lacking. So, give us the grace to do the very same. We pray for the American Church. Lord, teach us, as Paul said, to war a good warfare. Impart to us the balance of love and fierceness, gentleness and militancy, submission and tenacity, and show us how to intercept the insidious, ruthless, savage hordes of darkness through worship and intercession and spiritual warfare. Bring back a Church militantly victorious.

We ask You once again, Lord, to turn the tables on darkness. We pray that no longer will a second-rate, weaker power run roughshod, as if its open season over Christians. We acknowledge that because of our sins, according to Deuteronomy 32, there has been a reversal of the balance of power. How could one of the enemy chase a thousand, or two of the enemy put ten thousand of God's people to flight, ". . . **unless their Rock had sold them, unless the Lord had given them up?" (Deuteronomy 32:30)**

Lord, we repent and ask forgiveness for our rebellion, prayerlessness and idolatry. Restore true spiritual authority to the Church in Atlanta so that once again we would experience the exponential increase of power the way it was initially planned, so that one of us would put to flight a thousand of the enemy, two ten thousand, three a hundred thousand, four a million and seven a billion so that every time a brother or sister agrees with us in prayer the decimal is moved over one. Lord, give us this "decimal, decimating" power. Raise up these kind of intercessors and prayer groups in Atlanta. Thank You,

Lord, for being the Lamb of God and the Lion of Judah. This is the day the Lord has made. We shall rejoice and be glad in it.

In Jesus' name, amen.

Additional Scripture References

Proverbs 24:3-6
By wisdom a house is built, and through understanding it is established; through knowledge its rooms are filled with rare and beautiful treasures. A wise man has great power, and a man of knowledge increases strength; for waging war you need guidance, and for victory many advisers.

Proverbs 24:10-14
If you falter in times of trouble, how small is your strength! Rescue those being led away to death; hold back those staggering toward slaughter. If you say, "But we knew nothing about this," does not he who weighs the heart perceive it? Does not he who guards your life know it? Will he not repay each person according to what he has done? Eat honey, my son, for it is good; honey from the comb is sweet to your taste. Know also that wisdom is sweet to your soul; if you find it, there is a future hope for you, and your hope will not be cut off.

~7~

Prayer for
Those Who Stand in the Gap

Lord, today we are standing in the gap and making up the hedge for those who themselves have been standing in the gap for a long time, praying diligently for their loved ones, claiming healing deliverance, praying for spouses, children, for a job, finances, business, ministry, another home or a breakthrough in any area. We have assembled today to hold up their hands and ask You that these next few moments count for eternity. Let there be an unusual orchestration of praying saints all over metro Atlanta and let this end up being a mini-concert of prayer which will result in powerful testimonies which will resound to the glory of God.

Let the way of the Lord be prepared. Let the deck be cleared so we can pray effectual, fervent prayers that avail much. If anyone listening needs to search out someone and ask their forgiveness, give them the strength to do just that and not put it off another day. Let them not gloss over it or put it on the back burner. Pierce them, Lord, with intense conviction. Show them how vitally important relationships are in the Body of Christ. Don't let unforgiveness short-circuit their lives one more day. Let what happens today be so powerful

35

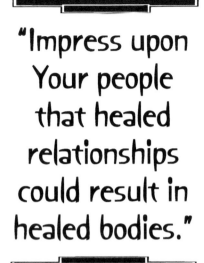

"Impress upon Your people that healed relationships could result in healed bodies."

that it will result in restoration and healing in the Body of Christ.

Impress upon Your people that healed relationships could result in healed bodies. Forgive us for even momentarily agreeing with and strengthening satan's hand or being one of his supporters by being used as an accuser of the brethren. Lord, for this we repent and ask Your forgiveness and cleansing by the precious Blood of Jesus.

We thank You that You promised us in Isaiah 58, if we would meet Your simple conditions, fast and pray, and cease the pointing of the finger, criticism, accusing one another, incredible things would begin to burst forth in our lives and we claim them right now for everyone listening. Let there be a fresh anointing behind the praying of this Scripture for everyone listening and help us to put away criticism and the pointing of the finger so these things can be real in our lives. By the grace of the living God, we will meet the conditions in Isaiah 58 and enter into these blessings:

- To loosen the chains of injustice
- To untie the cords of the yoke
- To set the oppressed free and break every yoke
- Your light will break forth like the dawn and your healing will quickly appear

- Your righteousness will go before you and the glory of the Lord will be your rear guard
- You will call and the Lord will answer
- You will cry for help and He will say, "Here am I"
- Your light will rise in the darkness and Your night will become like the noonday
- The Lord will guide you always
- He will satisfy your needs in a sun-scorched land and will strengthen your frame
- You will be like a well-watered garden, like a spring whose waters never fail
- Your people will rebuild the ancient ruins and will raise up the age-old foundations
- You will be called repairer of the broken walls, restorer of streets with dwellings
- You will find your joy in the Lord and He will cause you to ride on the heights of the land and to feast on the inheritance of your father Jacob—the mouth of the Lord has spoken

Now, we pray a special impartation of strength to Your people listening. Let a supernatural encouragement descend upon them. Come, Lord Jesus, today, banish far from them debilitating, paralyzing depression. Burst every yoke of bondage. Cut the chains. Loose them from their prison cell. Deliver them from mental anguish. We intercept the whisperings of the evil one. Those who right now can't quit crying, they are so burdened and tormented, we tell the powers of darkness to back off. Cease and desist your evil malignant work on God's children. Be gone! How dare you vex the servant of the Most High God! How dare you touch God's anointed! You have met more than your match. We proclaim in the sight of God and witnesses that the Blood of Jesus is against you, darkness, and the Blood of Jesus Christ is for every one of Your children listening this morning.

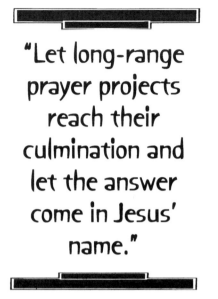

"Let long-range prayer projects reach their culmination and let the answer come in Jesus' name."

We claim Your Word in Psalm 30:5, *"For his anger lasts only a moment, but his favor lasts a lifetime; weeping may remain for a night, but rejoicing comes in the morning."* Come, Lord Jesus, be so personal and intimate with these people. Dry their tears. Be the lifter of their heads. Take them in Your arms. Embrace them. Let them know they are accepted in the Beloved and that You love them unconditionally. Assure them right now that You will never, ever leave them nor forsake them. Let there be such a presence of the Lord that they will know this day is their last lonely, lonesome day.

We pray that this day, their long night of weeping will come to an end and they will enter into Your morning of joy and rejoicing, and all of a sudden the veil is removed and they will move into a whole new dimension of walking with You, hearing the voice of the Father, praying powerful prayers that avail much and seeing the hand of the living God intervene in every area of their lives. Bring them from the land of captivity across the river into the Promised Land and let there be a celebration. Restore to them the joy of Your salvation so they can teach transgressors Your ways. Let the joy of the Lord once again be their strength.

"Lift up your heads, O you gates; be lifted up, you ancient doors, that the King of glory may come in.

Who is this King of glory? The Lord strong and mighty, the Lord mighty in battle.

Lift up your heads, O you gates; lift them up, you ancient doors, that the King of glory may come in.

Who is he, this King of glory? The Lord Almighty—he is the King of glory."

Psalm 24:7-10

Lord, we pray right now, that every gate in our lives will be completely opened up so the King of Glory may come in. Let this be a pivotal, banner week. Let this be a time of unprecedented breakthrough. We pray that prayers over the months and years could be amalgamated into a piercing laser beam prayer and that the answer that has been sought for such a long period of time will suddenly come—this week. We claim Your Word in the last verse of Isaiah 60:22, in Your time, You said You would do it suddenly. For many of Your children, this is the Kairos time.

Let the healing that is waiting in the wings swoop down and permeate hurting, diseased bodies with resurrection power, the same power that raised Christ Jesus from the dead. Let long-range prayer projects reach their culmination and let the answer come in Jesus' name. Let that great reservoir in heaven, spoken of in Revelation 5, which contains the prayers of the saints mixed with sweet incense, let it overflow, and what is happening in the heavens, let it pour down quickly on earth. Your will be done on earth as it is in heaven.

We claim the Scripture in Isaiah 35:3-6.

"Strengthen the feeble hands, steady the knees that give way;

say to those with fearful hearts, 'Be strong, do not fear; your God will come, he will come with vengeance; with divine retribution he will come to save you.'

Then will the eyes of the blind be opened and the ears of the deaf unstopped.

Then will the lame leap like a deer, and the mute tongue shout for joy. Water will gush forth in the wilderness and streams in the desert."

Lord, for those living in a dry and thirsty, barren, parched land, right now, let this very Word be rhema to them. Let it be quickened to them, out of the sun-baked, parched, desert land where they are right now, cause water to gush forth in their wilderness and streams in their desert.

We pray now an impartation of supernatural resilience and strength to press in, to hang on, for those who have taken hold of the horns of the altar and are fighting for theirs or others' lives. Lord, let this not be another perfunctory prayer like the ones prayed in dull, boring church services. Let the unction of heaven be on these prayers. Let the breath of God grace our requests.

Come, Lord Jesus. Rend the heavens. Come down. For many listening, time is of the essence. Some of Your children, as we speak, are desperate and desperately need a breakthrough. We celebrate You this day as the God of the breakthrough. You are well able to do exceedingly abundantly above all we ask or think. We lay claim to Jeremiah 33:3, *"Call to me and I will answer you and tell you great and unsearchable things you do not know."*

We invite You, Lord, to change our minds, change our perspective on life, change our outlook, alter our direction if necessary. Help us to do an about face and let there be a major metamorphosis in our lives. Upset the status quo. Lift us out of our ruts. Give us fresh motivation to seek Your face more than ever before. Let the fire of God fall upon us. Change our appetites. Give victory over carnal desires which are deteriorating and impart to us an insatiable thirst for fellowship with You and Your Word. Make us men and women of God, men and women of prayer, men and women of faith, men and women of the Word. Forgive us for thinking and uttering words of doubt, unbelief and questioning You. Let faith loom large in our lives. Help us to live by faith, to walk by faith, to speak faith and to think faith. We ask You this day to bring someone that will speak edifying, reinforcing, encouraging, anointed words to those out there who are in the depths of despair and struggling with life itself.

Lord, give them Your perspective. Help them to realize that *"the path of the righteous is like the first gleam of dawn, shining ever brighter till the full light of day" (Proverbs 4:18),* that though they stumble, they will not fall, for the Lord upholds him with His hand (Psalm 37:24). We pray for those who are going through severe trials and being sifted as wheat, just as Peter was. And Lord, we pray the same prayer for them that You prayed for Peter, that in this fiery ordeal their faith would not fail, and when this is over, You would be so redemptive to them, give them a large measure of grace, and they would turn and strengthen their brothers and sisters.

Thank You that this morning Your mercies were brand new. Thank You that this day You load us with benefits. Thank You, Lord, that what the enemy meant for evil, as we speak, You are turning it into good. Thank You, Lord, You are restoring the years where all these evil insects have eaten and You are rejuvenating Your children with nothing less than resurrection power. We celebrate You as the God of miracles.

Come, Lord Jesus. Show Yourself strong to Your servants. Press these battles to the gates. We dedicate this day to You. Let this be one of the most powerful weeks we have ever experienced in the Lord.

In Jesus' name, amen.

~8~

Prayer for
a "Jeremiah" Anointing

Dear Lord, we worship You, we adore You. You are worthy of all our praise. We extol You and exalt You to a high place. Be honored this day and we ask You to turn us into worshippers. Replace grumbling, murmuring, complaining, accusation and heaviness with a garment of praise. Let a mantle of worship descend on us today which will minister to You, bring You great joy, and at the same time, contribute to the revolutionizing of our lives, changing our mindsets, turning our captivities, restoring our fortunes, bring restoration, and if we're known for anything, let us be known as lavish worshippers of our Lord and Savior, Jesus Christ.

Lord, help us to pray prayers that avail much. Etch it deep into our hearts that the effectual fervent prayer of a righteous person avails very, very much. We ask You, Lord, to get us into such a place of intercession, that we could corporately pray concerning the state of our city or nation one day, and see the effects of our prayers in the next morning's newspaper. Forgive us for having made peace with mediocrity. Forgive us for wasting our times in unanointed, sterile, predictable meetings, singing the first, second and last.

Spare us from any more religious exercises in futility.

In the place of perfunctory, mundane, anemic, ho-hum meetings, we ask You to turn the Church of the Lord Jesus Christ in this city into an executive body which will corporately decree a thing, catapult forth that decree into the heavenlies, and see the staggering, mind-boggling extrapolation of exponential "decimal, decimating" prayer power—one of us will put to flight a thousand, two—ten thousand, four—a million, and seven a billion. We pray that once again in history, a second-rate diabolical power which for decades has run roughshod over the Church as if it were open season on Christians, would all of a sudden realize that his satanic heiness has met more than his match, is having eviction papers served on him, reels backward in abject panic and horror, and is routed out of this city into dry places to await the Judgment Day. Let it be that once again the Church has the initiative, the scepter is placed firmly in Its hands, the ball is in Its court. The Church speaks. The demonic nobilities must listen. The Church acts and darkness finds itself reacting.

Lord, we are serious. Whatever it takes, we pray for a Jeremiah anointing spoken of in Jeremiah 1:10, to root out, pull down, to destroy and overthrow that which is religious, fleshly, carnal and ecclesiastical, so that You can build and plant Your true New Testament Church. Let the Church in Atlanta begin to read like the Church in the book of Acts. Therefore, by the authority of the immutable Word of the living God, we ask You to root out spirits of religion, sectarianism, humanistic psychology, co-dependent groups, therapy sessions, etc., etc., and reduce the Church back down to the simplicity which is in Christ Jesus and return us back to our primary calling and initial mandate, that if the Church is known for anything, It is to be known as a House of Prayer for all nations. This year change the Church from religion to intimate relationship with Their God.

We ask You, Lord, to raise up intercessors who know what it means to leave their couches of comfort, and their laps of luxury, and their sitcom, soap-opera lifestyles, take up their crosses daily, pay the price, follow You, and stand in the gap and make up the hedge when lives are hanging in the balance, and see firebrands plucked from the burning.

Lord, our children need to witness what happened in David Edward's day, and George Finney's day and George Whitefield's day. They need to witness hardhearted, stone-cold, indifferent, depraved, wicked men and women stumbling into our services, and as soon as they cross the threshold, because the meetings have been so soaked in prayer, and the presence of the Lord is so profuse, they come under strong, piercing, intense conviction, begin to weep, cry out to God for mercy and forgiveness, fall on their knees in repentance, and come up marvelously, radically saved.

> **"This year change the Church from religion to intimate relationship with Their God."**

We ask You, Lord, to give this city compassionate, anointed askers and seekers who will persevere until the answer comes, who will pray earthshaking, devil-disturbing, death-defying prayers over this city and over this nation. We ask You, Holy Spirit of the living God, to call the Church of Atlanta and America back to its moorings, back to its sanity,

"As we worship You, release that anointing that is invisible, but is perceptible."

back to the Bible, back to its Judeo-Christian roots, back to its knees and back to its God. Bring back old-fashioned solemn assemblies. Let the call go out all over this world-class city for battle-ready, compassionate, seasoned, green-beret veterans of the faith prayer warriors who are loving, militant and tenacious, who will not take "no" for an answer, and who will take an assignment all the way to the gates. By the grace of the living God, we're going to pray relentlessly, perseveringly, until principalities and powers are pulled down and the Spirit of the Lord moves across this nation with a tidal wave of revival. Bring glory back into Your Church.

We thank You, Lord, that whatever happened in Early Awakenings and revivals, that during the last great harvest, there is going to be a historically unprecedented spiritual awakening that will shake this city and this nation. Thank You, Lord, that the glory of the latter house will greatly exceed that of the former. Thank You that the knowledge of the glory of the Lord will cover the earth as the waters cover the sea. Thank You, Lord, that You promised that even greater things than You did will we do and thank You, Lord, that You have saved the best wine till last. We are going to praise You morning, noon and night.

Once again, we pray that You would make us like Abraham, who not only worshipped You, but it became his lifestyle. His life actually was a worship, and wherever he went, except when he detoured down into Egypt, he left a trail of altars. Let it be that wherever we go, we will leave a trail of altars and indelible marks on people's lives. Like it was said of Abraham, let it be said of us, that he staggered not because he gave glory to God. As we worship You, release that anointing that is invisible, but is perceptible. It's like perfume. It's a savor that Scripture says ministers death to demon spirits of death, and ministers life to those who have the Spirit of life—wherever we go.

We thank You for Your promise in Isaiah 42:10-13.

"Sing to the Lord a new song, his praise from the ends of the earth, you who go down to the sea, and all that is in it, you islands, and all who live in them.

Let the desert and its towns raise their voices; let the settlements where Kedar lives rejoice. Let the people of Sela sing for joy; let them shout from the mountaintops.

Let them give glory to the Lord and proclaim his praise in the islands.

The Lord will march out like a mighty man, like a warrior he will stir up his zeal; with a shout he will raise the battle cry and will triumph over his enemies."

In the name of Jesus, amen.

~9~

Prayer for
Celebrating the Resurrection
Power of Jesus Christ

Dear Lord, as we pray these prayers, help us to meet Your simple conditions. Let there be a melt-down of our hearts. We relinquish all resentment, bitterness, anger, and we readily forgive anyone who has ever hurt, abused, or stolen from us, and since we have the power either to retain or remit, we choose to remit and release them so that many of these perpetrators can come into Your kingdom and experience Your forgiveness. God forbid that we would ever be turned over to the tormentors, as Jesus taught in one of His parables, because we have been forgiven so much and refuse to forgive so little in comparison. We pray for a revival of forgiveness to spread over greater Atlanta.

We thank You for a glorious Easter day and we continue to celebrate the resurrection power of Jesus Christ. We pray that every day this year would be Easter in our hearts and that the life of the Lord would flow freely, profusely, unhindered, like a cascading river of pure water. We pray a fresh anointing in our lives. For those who have lost the lustre, the fervor, the zest, the enthusiasm of fellowshipping with You, we ask You to put them back on the cutting edge of walking in the Spirit and being up-to-date with what You are doing and saying. Help us to be like the children of Issachar who knew what season they were in, had an understanding of their times and knew what to do in that season. We pray Galatians 5:25.

"Since we live by the Spirit, let us keep in step with the Spirit."

We pray for religious people that they would forsake their dead, dull, boring, perfunctory religion and cease wasting time in ecclesiastical exercises in futility and come into an intimate, passionate, vital, living relationship with the Lord Jesus Christ. We pray as David did in Psalm 63:1, 2,

"O God, you are my God, earnestly I seek you; my soul thirsts for you, my body longs for you, in a dry and weary land where there is no water.

I have seen you in the sanctuary and beheld your power and your glory."

We pray according to the calling on Jeremiah to root out, tear down, pluck and destroy lifeless religion which has no anointing, and to plant and build Your true Church which flows freely with the power and love of the Lord Jesus Christ. Where the Spirit of the Lord is, there is liberty.

For those right now who can't even identify with Easter, who are in the depths of despair, paralyzed by depression, covered with a cloud of confusion, questioning the reality of life itself, we ask You, Lord, to come, invade their vehicles, their homes, their hospital rooms, their prisons, their lives. Come Lord Jesus, show Yourself so strong to these individuals and let this be a day of deliverance for them. We claim one of the greatest Easter passages which says that "if that same Spirit which raised Christ Jesus from the dead dwells inside of you, it shall quicken your mortal bodies." Lord, we present to You the pain-wracked, crippled, disease-ridden bodies of those who are listening right now and their loved ones. We lay them on Your altar.

Come Lord Jesus, as people out there are desperately hanging on and hoping against hope for the healing that is waiting in the wings, let it swoop down and inundate

"Remove the dreariness of just existing and impart to them Godly gusto and resurrection power."

their feeble bodies. Let that same power that raised Christ from the grave permeate their lives, radically touch every cell of their bodies, penetrate every fiber of their beings, bring healing, strength, renewal, restore the years where the demonic insects, cankerworm, palmer worm, caterpillar and locust have eaten. On their behalf, as a corporate interceding body, in a concert of prayer, we lay claim to Your infallible, unchanging Word which is forever settled in heaven. By Your wounds and by Your stripes, we avail ourselves of healing that has already been provided at the cross.

We apply the precious blood of Jesus to their bodies. Raise them up. Make them every whit whole. Transform them into a living, walking, astounding testimony which will resound to Your glory. We rejoice in the new season of spring. All around us we see the bursting forth of new, fresh life. We can't help but believe that there's a parallel in the natural and the spiritual, that for many out there who have been hanging in there, who have become survivors, they're desperately waiting to hear a Word from the Lord, we believe a new season is bursting open and You will not let them down. You're the God of times and season; You're the God of new beginnings.

Encourage Your people that help is on the way. We appropriate this Word for them from Isaiah 42:16.

"I will lead the blind by ways they have not known, along unfamiliar paths I will guide them; I will turn the darkness into light before them and make the rough places smooth. These are the things I will do; I will not forsake them."

Lord, You are the Great Potentate. You are an awesome God. To You we ascribe honor, glory and majesty forever. Amen. Be the God of faith and hope to everyone listening. Remove the dreariness of just existing and impart to them Godly gusto and resurrection power. In Jesus' name, amen.

Additional Scripture References

John 14:6

Proverbs 21:16 (Amplified)

Romans 8:6

John 1:4

Acts 1:3

John 10:10

Psalm 118:17

~10~

Prayer for
Becoming a Generation of Prayer

Thank You, Lord. You're not only our Redeemer, but You're incredibly redemptive. There is nothing You can't do—nothing, absolutely nothing is impossible with You. You're the God of the new beginning.

We celebrate You, Lord that when we are at the end of our rope, run totally out of options, expended all of our resources, bankrupted our humanistic think tanks, run head-on into a brick wall, become desperate, and time is of the essence, this is where You begin.

We're asking You, Lord, this day, that we don't pray weak, apologetic prayers, but we pray today, corporately, all over this city, in the inestimable power of prayer agreement, You would turn us into an executive body and we would send forth decrees into the heavenlies which would not cease nor desist until You, Lord, do Your Divine office work in our lives.

Psalm 68:1, 2
"May God arise, may his enemies be scattered; may his foes flee before him.

As smoke is blown away by the wind, may you blow them away; as wax melts before the fire, may the wicked perish before God."

We thank You, Lord, that even though darkness covers the earth, and gross darkness the people, the brilliant light of the Lord is rising upon Your Church. As this world system hemorrhages from perversion and staggers under the crushing load of demonic activity, satanism and wickedness, we thank You, Lord, that Your Church is coming into its finest hour. Right now, as we pray, give Your people Your perspective as to where we are in history. We thank You that where sin abounds, in direct proportion, Your grace does all that much more abound.

This is the generation of prayer. Lord, help us to heed I Peter 4:7.

"The end of all things is near. Therefore be clear minded and self-controlled so that you can pray."

We realize throughout history that every spiritual awakening has been preceded by a mighty revival of prayer. We thank You, Lord, that history is about to repeat itself. For the last 300 years, we have had a major war in the sixties, and a historic revival at the turn of the century and we're on the threshold of the greatest awakening America has even known.

We beseech You, Lord. Raise up an army of green-beret remnant intercessors who are in their element when they pray—loving, compassionate, caring, have the capacity to weep over a city like You did, and also are militant, tenacious, warring, invincible, and just two or three of them in agreement become a formidable foe against darkness. Lord, raise up prayer warriors who won't take "no" for an answer, even when logic, circumstances, evidence and reports scream out against

54

them. Give us pray-ers who are not unnerved by the rattling of satan's saber, who know how to stand in the gap, make up the hedge, take hold of the horns of the altar, and as Joel says, who weep between the altar and the porch, and take an assignment all the way to the gates.

Lord, raise up a praying Church Who will strike abject terror into the heart of darkness, serve eviction papers on satan's military command—all the way from private, corporal demons, up to diabolical generals, principalities, powers, territorial spirits, demonic nobilities and his satanic heiness himself. Let his evilness know he has met more than his match. Greater is He that is within us than he that is in the world. Give these pray-ers the fortitude and courage to say, as Job said, "satan, you may have come this far, you're not coming any further."

> "Lord, raise up prayer warriors who won't take "no" for an answer, . . ."

God, give us prayer warriors who will not make peace with mediocrity, who have keen discernment, can smell a religious spirit a mile away, and never again will waste their precious time in unanointed religious exercises in futility. Give us ones whose heads are not turned by the smell of money, who have no price tags hanging off of them. They can't be bought, leveraged, manipulated or controlled. Intercessors who when they go out to the battlefield have spiritual authority on their heads because they're under spiritual authority and are covered by their local church body.

> "Give us ones [prayer-ers] whose heads are not turned by the smell of money, who have no price tags hanging off of them."

Lord, give us prevailing pray-ers who move in such anointed power that they will pray one evening for a critical situation and see the result of their prayers in the next morning's headlines. Raise up interveners who so meet Your conditions, that when they assemble for prayer, they are turned into an executive body to send forth decrees into the heavenlies which will not cease nor desist until You, Lord, do Your sovereign office work.

We pray for the same breed of intercessors like Father Clery and Father Nash who accompanied Charles Finney to his meetings, and along with other spiritual movers and shakers, that through their prayers brought about such a transformation in their day that there were areas of the city one could not possibly go through without becoming radically born again.

It's harvest time. We can hear the rustling of Your garments over Atlanta and America. Thank You, Lord for:

- the 160 million Christians praying for revival
- the 10 million prayer groups around the world
- the 36 million who are praying regularly for the 10-40 window
- the 3 million children and teenagers who prayed at the flagpole last year, and

♦ the 1.1 million fathers and husbands who attended *Promise Keepers* in 1996

Thank You that the glory of the latter house will greatly exceed that of the former. Thank You that the knowledge of the glory of the Lord will cover the earth as the waters cover the sea. Thank You that You are pouring out Your Spirit on all flesh and You have saved the best wine till last.

Lord, whatever You do, return the American Church back to its original mandate and destiny—if it is known for anything, let it be known primarily as a House of Prayer for all nations.

I Peter 4:7
"The end of all things is near. Therefore be clear minded and self-controlled so that you can pray."

In Jesus' name, amen.

Additional Scripture References

Jeremiah 29:11-13
"For I know the plans I have for you," declares the Lord, "plans to prosper you and not to harm you, plans to give you hope and a future. Then you will call upon me and come and pray to me, and I will listen to you. You will seek me and find me when you seek me with all your heart."

I John 5:14, 15
This is the confidence we have in approaching God: that if we ask anything according to his will, he hears us. And if we know that he hears us—whatever we ask—we know that we have what we asked of him.

Philippians 4:6
Do not be anxious about anything, but in everything by prayer and petition, with thanksgiving, present your requests to God.

~ 11 ~

Prayer for the Restoration of Proper Stewardship to the Church

Lord, we ask You this morning to prepare our hearts for the visitation of Your Spirit which has been promised in Scripture. Like Daniel when he discovered through the Word that the seventy years of desolation of Jerusalem would come to an end, he didn't just sit back and watch history roll. He entered into fervent, effectual, travailing prayer, with all of his heart, to pray in the purposes, times and seasons of the Lord (Daniel 9:1-19). So, Lord, help us by Your Spirit to do likewise. As Paul stated, we are praying to fill up that which is lacking and return Your Church back to the simplicity which is in Christ Jesus (Colossians 1:24).

We agree together today on behalf of the Church of the Lord Jesus Christ. Thank You that as we fervently pray, You are restoring, adjusting and dealing with the blind spots in Your Church. Open our eyes to true New Testament Church. Give us the resolve to separate ourselves from those who "have a form of godliness, but deny the power thereof," (2 Timothy 3:5) and let our gatherings begin to resemble the New Testament and read like the Church in the book of Acts.

Your Word says that when we repent, You would bring seasons of refreshing (Acts 3:19). We repent, Lord, of our complacent, apathetic, attitude. Lift us off our laps of luxury, our couches of comfort. Blast us out of our comfort zones and our desire to gratify the flesh with inordinate self-aggrandizement. Forgive us of being lovers of pleasure more than lovers of God. Forgive us for perpetuating gross inequities in the Church which have padded the religious coffers of the ecclesiastical, traditional Church, with all its ornate architecture and palatial buildings, while true, called, anointed servants of the Lord barely eke out a livelihood. We thank You, Lord, through prayer, You're dealing with this inconsistent travesty in the Church.

We repent of the lust of the flesh, the lust of the eyes and the pride of life (1 John 2:16), our haughty attitudes and arrogant ways. Lord, forgive the Church in Atlanta and America for breathing in the anesthesia of the spirit of this age and lapsing into a state of spiritual stupor, and not being mesmerized by the cutting edge of what the Spirit of God is doing and saying.

"Blast us out of our comfort zones and our desire to gratify the flesh with inordinate self-aggrandizement."

Forgive us, Lord, for having our priorities out of order and for losing our first love. Do not spew us out of Your mouth. Give us more time. Stir the embers which are barely glowing, which are about to smoke and be extinguished, and re-ignite in us a passion for the Lord Jesus Christ as we have never known in our entire lifetime. Help us to realize that the only thing that is going to accomplish the purposes of God in our life, in this city, in this nation is the zeal of the Lord of hosts.

Let it be said of us that our magnificent obsession is the Lord Jesus Christ. Re-instill into us, Lord, such a passion to seek Your face, eat Your Word, drink at Your fountain, banquet at Your table, to come aside and enter into Your inner sanctum, to enter into the Holy of Holies with You, that like David, we'll hardly be able to wait and will say, "When can we come and spend intimate time with You?" Lord, let us so experience this that the hours with You and Your Word would seem like minutes.

Thank You, Lord, You are restoring reciprocity back to the Church. Thank You, Lord, for Your Word which is effective in this day of awakening,

Psalm 110:3 (KJV)
"Thy people shall be willing *[volunteer freely]* **in the day of thy power. . . ."**

Thank You, Lord, that the new covenant is greater than the old covenant, and if they had to convince the people in the Old Testament to stop giving because they had so much, eventually, we will have that same problem in the New Testament.

Help Your people to sow into where they are receiving anointed ministry, whether it's tax-deductible or not. Help them to realize that indeed the laborer is worthy of his hire, the worker deserves his wages, and those who receive instruction in the Word share all good things with their teacher, contributing to their support.

Eradicate from our minds an "Americanized, architectural" mindset which places premiums on stained glass windows, steeples and ornate Gothic finery, to the neglect of the support of Your anointed servants. Open our eyes to what true New Testament "ekklesia" really is. Open the floodgate of resources to adequately support the anointed, intercessory, prophetic ministries which You are now raising up in Your Church. Thank You that the "glory of the latter house will greatly exceed that of the former" (Haggai 2:9). Thank You that the effectual, fervent prayer of a righteous person avails very, very much.

In Jesus' name, we pray. Amen.

~12~

Prayer for Protection Over Our Cities

Dear Lord, we approach You this morning, humbling confessing our sins. Search our hearts. We want to be up-to-date with You and one another as we approach Your throne so we can pray effective prayers. We invite You, Lord, to move invisibly in Holiness in our lives so that You can move visibly with power in the Church and in this city. Cleanse us by the power that is in the Blood of Jesus Christ and by the washing of the Word. Though our sins be as scarlet, make them white as snow.

We ask You, these next few moments, to orchestrate a concert of prayer among hundreds, possibly thousands, of intercessors to beseech You to have mercy upon our great city. The effectual, fervent prayer of a righteous person avails much.

God, hasten the day that we no longer have a spiritual vacuum into which rushes every imaginably perverse thing, nearly unhindered or unrestrained, as if it were open season. Turn back the horde of evil that has infiltrated our city. Ring this entire area with strong angels with blazing, two-edged swords.

Let God arise so thoroughly in this metropolitan area that diabolical powers will be throttled down, neutralized, rendered powerless, and bound with cords dipped in the Blood of Jesus Christ. Silence evil so it will not bluster about pontificating in such an arrogant manner. Let righteousness rule and reign. Come, Prince of Peace, usher in the Lordship of Jesus Christ within our borders. Lift up your heads, O you gates, be lifted up you ancient doors; that the King of Glory may come in. Who is this King of Glory? The Lord strong and mighty, the Lord mighty in battle.

We claim Your Word that says, when the enemy comes in like a flood, You will raise up a standard against him. Deliver us and rescue us from the hands of spiritual foreigners whose mouths are full of lies, whose right hands are deceitful, so that there will be no breaching of walls, no going into captivity, no cry of distress in our streets.

We ask You, Lord, to move in a sovereign, decisive way. Help us to drop our anchor and set our faces as flint. We are going to pray until this city becomes a safe haven and a city of refuge. We believe, just as this city was once ravaged by Sherman's fire during the Civil War, so once again, You are going to rend the heavens, respond to our pleas, sweep through this greater metropolitan area with another fire, the fire of the Holy Spirit of God. Let it be as if we can hear the rustling of Your garments going in and out of thoroughfares, neighborhoods, homes, businesses, schools, lives, homes, marriages, children.

Wake up a slumbering Church. Sound the trumpet. Alert the watchmen on the wall. Bring us into a state of readiness. Descend upon us with the Dove of Your Spirit and the mantle of intercession. Give us the grace to pray and pray and pray until the shout of victory is heard in the camp. We offer ourselves as candidates for night seasons, to walk with You in the midnight hour or early morning, to be faithful in the night watches.

By Your grace and strength, we want to move into a stance of preparedness and vigilance

"Wake up a slumbering Church."

to seek Your face until we see You burst on the scene and respond to the desperate pleas of Your servants. Visit our city. Plunder the camp of the Egyptians. Grace us with the magnificent splendor of Your light. Let darkness become disoriented. Bring confusion into the camp of evil. Cause them to turn one against another.

Tear down the walls of division. Bring about a spirit of unity. Raise up a city-wide Church to win a city-wide war. Raise up prayer warriors. Extend Your mighty scepter from Zion. Rule in the midst of Your enemies. Give us the grace to eat at Your table that is spread for us in the midst of our enemies, then give us a fresh anointing. Anoint our heads with fresh oil.

We beseech You, Lord, to raise up a choir of worshippers, who, like in Jehoshaphat's day, will enter into warfare worship. Let the high praises of God be in our mouth to the extent that while we worship, just like when You went out with armies in days of old, You will set ambushments for the evil one and deliver the righteous. We pray, Lord, You would not be appalled at the lack of intercessors, nor let not justice be driven back, nor righteousness stand at a distance, nor truth stumble in the streets, nor honesty be hindered from entering. We make a strong plea to bring forth righteousness, justice and equity.

Even when they return at evening, snarling like dogs, and prowl about the city, wandering about for food and howling because of dissatisfaction, we will sing of Your strength. In the morning we will sing of Your love; for You are our fortress, our refuge in times of trouble. O Lord, our strength, we sing praises to You; You, O God are our fortress, our loving God.

"We ask You, Lord, to bring into our lives a Divine dissatisfaction with the way things are."

Lord God, help us to have the Divine capacity, at the appointed moment, to be as gentle, loving, compassionate, harmless and tender as a lamb, and when You give the signal to go to war, to have the flexibility of new wineskins to shift into the mode of fierce, militant warrior and storm the gates of hell, so that Your kingdom can be advanced, Your will be done on earth as it is in heaven. Captives can be set free, the maimed, halted, withered and diseased can be healed. Help us at that moment to become spiritually violent and take the kingdom of heaven by force.

We ask You, Lord, to bring into our lives a Divine

dissatisfaction with the way things are. God forbid that we settle down for the status quo. For Atlanta's sake, we will not keep silent, until her righteousness shines out like the dawn, her salvation like a blazing torch.

We praise You for the opportunity to agree in prayer. We are going to celebrate You morning, noon and night. Our heart is full of gratitude for Your mercies are new every morning. Thank You, Lord, for all You've done and all that is in the process in the heavenlies this morning. Press this battle to the gates. You are a great God. Thank You, Lord. Have mercy upon our city.

In Jesus' name, Amen.

Additional Scripture References

Psalm 59

Deliver me from my enemies, O God; protect me from those who rise up against me. Deliver me from evildoers and save me from bloodthirsty men. See how they lie in wait for me! Fierce men conspire against me for no offense or sin of mine, O Lord. I have done no wrong, yet they are ready to attack me. Arise to help me; look on my plight! O Lord God Almighty, the God of Israel, rouse yourself to punish all the nations; show no mercy to wicked traitors. They return at evening, snarling like dogs, and prowl about the city. See what they spew from their mouths—they spew out swords from their lips, and they say, "Who can hear us?" But you, O Lord, laugh at them; you scoff at all those nations. O my Strength, I watch for you; you, O God, are my fortress, my loving God. God will go before me and will let me gloat over those who slander me. But do not kill them, O Lord our shield, or my people will forget. In your might make them wander about, and bring them down. For the sins of their mouths, for the words of their lips, let them be caught in their pride. For the curses and lies they utter, consume them in wrath, consume them till they are no more. Then it will be known to the ends of the earth that God rules over Jacob. They return at evening, snarling like dogs, and prowl about the city. They wander about for food and howl if not satisfied. But I will sing of your strength, in the morning I will sing of your love; for you are my fortress, my refuge in times of trouble. O my Strength, I sing praises to you; you, O God, are my fortress, my loving God.

Psalm 144:5-15

Part your heavens, O Lord, and come down; touch the mountains, so that they smoke. Send forth lightning and scatter the enemies; shoot your arrows and rout them. Reach down your hand from on high; deliver me and rescue me from the mighty waters, from the hands of foreigners whose mouths are full of lies, whose right hands are deceitful. I will sing a new song to you, O God; on the ten-stringed lyre I will make music to you, to the One who gives victory to kings, who delivers his servant David from the deadly sword. Deliver me and rescue me from the hands of foreigners whose mouths are full of lies, whose right hands are deceitful. Then our sons in their youth will be like well-nurtured plants, and our daughters will be like pillars carved to adorn a palace. Our barns will be filled with every kind of provision. Our sheep will increase by thousands, by tens of thousands in our fields; our oxen will draw heavy loads. There will be no breaching of walls, no going into captivity, no cry of distress in our streets. Blessed are the people of whom this is true; blessed are the people whose God is the Lord.

~13~

Prayer for Forgiveness for Our Prayerlessness

Dear Lord, today we set our faces like flint to seek You. Let the slate be clean in our lives this morning. Let us not try to function this week without being cleansed by the powerful Blood of Jesus Christ. We want to be up-to-date with You and with each other. We lay claim to Your precious promise that if we confess our sins, You are faithful and just to forgive us our sins and cleanse us from all unrighteousness. Though our sins be as scarlet, though some may have gone into the depths of sin and wonder if they have gone too far, let them know that there is nothing that Your Blood cannot cleanse. There's not a pit too deep that You cannot retrieve them from. Though our sins be as scarlet, You can make them as white as snow.

We once again celebrate You today as not only our Redeemer, but You are incredibly redemptive. You buy back, You pull out of, You rescue from, You are the Great Restorer, and You said in Isaiah 58:12 that if we sought You, and fasted and prayed, that we would rebuild ancient ruins, raise up age-old foundations; and be called repairer of broken walls, restorer of streets with dwellings. Lord, we would love to be called just that—a rebuilder, repairer and restorer.

We pray that many testimonies today would be like that of David's in Psalm 40:1-3.

"I waited patiently for the Lord; he turned to me and heard my cry.

He lifted me out of the slimy pit, out of the mud and mire; he set my feet on a rock and gave me a firm place to stand.

He put a new song in my mouth, a hymn of praise to our God. Many will see and fear and put their trust in the Lord."

This morning, bring a season of refreshing on the Church of the Lord Jesus Christ in Atlanta, as we repent of prayerlessness. We acknowledge, Lord, that it is the most unused, untapped, unrealized, underestimated power in the whole universe. We not only repent and ask forgiveness for lack of prayer, but as a result of this, we repent of our sit-com, soap-opera lifestyles, being shallow and without substance, without guidance of the Holy Spirit, our church services being boring, mundane, redundant, predictable, like tinkling cymbal and sounding brass. Forgive us for having made peace with mediocrity. Forgive us, Lord, for prayerlessness which has resulted in powerlessness. Forgive us, Lord, for deteriorating into such mundane, bland church meetings that many of our young people have left them years ago to go to a second-rate power, satanism, to get their rush, their sense of power, and their identity.

Forgive us, Lord, for lack of intercessors as spoken of in Isaiah 59, which has resulted in the same conditions in Atlanta: Justice is driven back, righteousness stands at a distance, truth has stumbled in the streets, honesty cannot enter, truth is nowhere to be found, and whoever shuns evil, becomes a prey. Lord, we repent that You looked and were displeased because there was no justice, and You were appalled that there was no one to intercede. We realize, Lord, that according to Scripture, You are in a state of shock over the average American Church, for lack of corporate prayer.

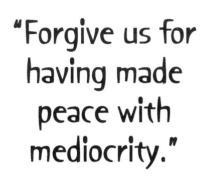

"Forgive us for having made peace with mediocrity."

Forgive us, Lord, for there being a dearth of corporate prayer in Atlanta. We have seemingly everything else. We are replete with concerts, libraries, fellowship halls, Sunday Schools, board meetings, strategy sessions, biblical analysis, scriptural outlines, ecclesiastical dialogues, seminary classes, religious activities, sewing circles, church bazaars, addicts anonymous, choir practices, music classes, church night suppers, co-dependent groups, self-help classes, psychological profiles, psychological counseling sessions, etc., etc.,—but we have precious little corporate prayer. Consequently, when the average American thinks of Church, they think of a building of brick and stone, not a dynamic group of called-out ones. Lord, change our mindsets. Remove the Americanized stereotyped, stigmatized version of Church, even the connotation of the word, and replace it with visions of a vibrant, powerful, anointed, unctionized, life-changing New Testament assembly like we read about in the book of Acts. Make us jealous for what we read about in history books concerning the Early Awakening and the Welsh revival. Make us jealous for what we read about in Scripture concerning the New Testament Church.

71

You never said, "My house shall be a house of preaching and teaching," as important as that is when it is anointed, but You said it should be known as a House of Prayer for all nations. You never taught Your disciples how to teach and preach, as important as that is under the anointing of the Holy Spirit, but You taught them how to pray. We confess to You this morning, that we are in desperate need of intercessors who know how to take a prayer project, and lovingly, tenaciously, militantly, set their faces like flint, storm the gates of heaven, and plunder the corridors of hell, and won't take "no" for an answer, but take an assignment all the way to the gates. Lord, teach us what it means that ever since John the Baptist, the violent take the kingdom of heaven by force.

> "Make us jealous for what we read about in Scripture concerning the New Testament Church."

Lord, we need intercessors who know what it means to leave their couches of comfort, and their laps of luxury, take up their crosses daily, follow You, and stand in the gap and make up the hedge when lives are hanging in the balance and see firebrands plucked from the burning. Lord, we desperately need prayer warriors who know what it means to take hold of the horns of the altar, weep between the altar and the porch as spoken of in Joel because of the desperate plight of their nation.

Lord, our children need to witness what happened in

David Edwards' day and George Finney's day and George Whitefield's day. Our children need to witness hard-hearted, stone-cold, indifferent, depraved, wicked men and women stumbling into our services, and as soon as they cross the threshold, because the meetings have been soaked in prayer, and the presence of the Lord is so profuse, they come under strong, piercing, intense conviction, begin to weep convulsively, cry out to God for mercy and forgiveness, fall on their knees in repentance, and come up marvelously, radically saved. Our children have not witnessed this in their lifetime. Lord, it's time that they see it. Whatever the cost, raise up intercessors. Bring a spiritual awakening that will sweep this city and this nation.

Lord, bring back ministry so bathed in prayer before, during, and after its delivery, that it will fulfill the only conditions upon which Your Word is to be preached as Paul stated in First Thessalonians 1:5,

". . .our gospel came to you not simply with words, but also with power, with the Holy Spirit and with deep conviction. . . ."

Let us be so convicted about this Lord, that we would cast aside the performance mentality, and not make a move, even though it's 11 AM Sunday morning and the pews are packed with people, until You, Lord, and Your powerful Spirit show up.

We repent on behalf of a large number of pastors who admitted, when questioned, that they spent four minutes per day in prayer. Lord, we ask You to make us like Elijah, who even though he got weary and discouraged, lonely, despised, betrayed, was no great success in any way except as a prophet, yet he was such a powerful man of prayer that he prayed it would not rain, and it didn't for three and a half years. He prayed again and it rained and the earth produced its crops.

Lord, forgive us for our spineless, wiener, milk-toast, wimpy, gutless leadership in some Atlanta churches who are politically and religiously correct, who act like hirelings, and who dish out Pablum to their congregation each Sunday morning. Forgive us, Lord, for being so prayerless and so unanointed that a large constituency of our congregations are depressed, sickly, weak, defeated, suicidal and demonized on a regular basis. Forgive us, Lord, that because of prayerlessness, we seldom see the supernatural, we hardly ever see signs following preaching to confirm the Word, the word "miraculous" has become controversial, and most Christians would be hard-pressed to distinguish between a civic club and the average church.

We pray in such oasis of prayer, that when people assemble, they would experience what it says in Isaiah 35:3-7, and that even now, You would touch Your people in this manner.

"Strengthen the feeble hands, steady the knees that give way;

say to those with fearful hearts, 'Be strong, do not fear; your God will come, he will come with vengeance; with divine retribution he will come to save you.'

Then will the eyes of the blind be opened and the ears of the deaf unstopped.

Then will the lame leap like a deer, and the mute tongue shout for joy. Water will gush forth in the wilderness and streams in the desert.

The burning sand will become a pool, the thirsty ground bubbling springs. . . ."

You are the God of the breakthroughs. You are the One Who can make everything new. You take away the stale and stagnant, and bring that which is new, fresh and revitalizing. You are the One, Who with one stroke of Your hand can banish far from us hopelessness and despair. Even though our society is rampant with it, even though it reeks with grumbling, murmuring, bad report, darkness, heaviness, depression, Lord, with the wind of Your Spirit, blow it out of our lives and replace it lavishly with the attributes of Your Spirit. And we speak these right now to Your people listening.

Receive from the hand of the Lord: love, joy, peace, acceptance, forgiveness, restoration, guidance, encouragement, edification, strength. Receive right now: hope, faith, good report of the Lord in place of bad report, joyful anticipation, healing, reinforcement, buoyancy, vision. God, let Your attributes replace those evil characteristics which have

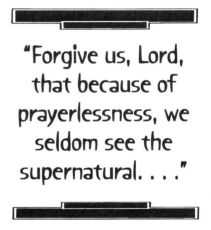

"Forgive us, Lord, that because of prayerlessness, we seldom see the supernatural. . . ."

crept in by the ether waves of this humanistic world system. Let us experience firsthand what Your Word says in Romans 12:2, that we no longer conform any longer to the pattern of this world, but be transformed by the renewing of our minds. Then we will be able to test and approve what God's will is, Your good and pleasing and perfect will.

In Jesus' name, amen.

Additional Scripture References

Isaiah 63:5
Psalm 79:6
Jeremiah 10:21; 25
Ezekiel 13:5 (KJV)
Job 21:14, 15
James 4:1, 2
Isaiah 59:14-16 (Amplified)
Psalm 14:4 (Amplified)
Ezekiel 22:30 (Amplified)
Isaiah 56:7 (Amplified)
Luke 18:1 (Amplified)

~14~

Prayer for the Renewal and Transformation of Our Minds

Dear Lord, we pray that these few moments would be some of the most powerful of this day, that this prayer agreement would launch the week, and we would find ourselves feasting at the table of the Lord. We pray that these next few days would be different from the others. We dedicate them right now to be set apart to the Lord so much so that we would look out on the horizon and see You approaching in a manner we have never experienced before.

Show Your people, right now, there is hope for them right where they are. You haven't forgotten their address. You have promised to never leave nor forsake them. You're never too late. There's still time. There's still hope. Your grace is still extended to them. They are the apple of Your eye and You are concentrating on them and their circumstances right now.

Come, Lord Jesus, rend the heavens. Come down and tabernacle with those who desperately need to hear from You and sense Your presence, in Jesus' name. God of all comfort, we ask You to gently descend like a cloud upon those who are hurting, suffering, in any kind of anguish or grief or despondency. Once again, replace a spirit of heaviness with a garment of praise. Let melodious worship burst forth from the downtrodden and rejected. We worship You, Lord. You are worthy to be praised. We pray that today, we would decrease and You would increase.

Forgive us all of our sins and help us at this moment to be up-to-date with You and with each other. Help us, as it says in First Corinthians 13 to not keep account of the bad things that people do to us. We throw that scorecard away, right now. Give us the grace to forbear and be patient and to understand and to put ourselves in other people's shoes, and extend grace, like You have extended it to us, and give breathing room. We pray that we would be known as dispensers of the grace of God. Grace and peace to You in Jesus' name.

Lord, we confess to You today that we are hungry and thirsty for more of You. The trinkets and toys and materialism of this world don't fulfill us. As David cried out in Psalm 63:1, 2,

"O God, you are my God, earnestly I seek you; my soul thirsts for you, my body longs for you, in a dry and weary land where there is no water.

I have seen you in the sanctuary and beheld your power and your glory."

Lord, we have been ruined. We have tasted of the new wine of Your Spirit. We have banqueted at Your table. We have partaken of Your bread. We have drunk at Your fountain. Nothing, absolutely nothing else, will satisfy. We have been spoiled for life.

For those who are bowed down because of stress and burdens, who are distracted and pre-occupied with difficult situations and problems which at this moment seem to be bigger than life itself and appear to be a large looming, insurmountable mountain that has no human answer, we pray that these dear people would avail for themselves of the Scripture Philippians 4:6, 7.

"Do not be anxious about anything, but in everything, by prayer and petition, with thanksgiving, present your requests to God.

And the peace of God, which transcends all understanding, will guard your hearts and your minds in Christ Jesus."

Also, Lord, we lay claim to the next verse, that we are going to fix our minds and think on whatever is true, whatever is noble, whatever is right, whatever is pure, whatever is lovely, whatever is admirable. If anything is excellent or praiseworthy, we are going to think about such things.

We ask You, Lord, to take control of our minds. We have decided not to be conformed to this world system, but rather to be transformed by the renewing of our minds. Remove every thought, regardless of how subtle it may be, every thought of doubt, unbelief, questioning, despair, hopelessness, every thought that says, "I can't", and replace it with the assurance from the Lord that "I can do all things through Christ which strengtheneth me." In the place of doubt and unbelief, we are going to walk in faith, speak in faith, act in faith, and by the grace of God, be pried loose from our rut and pit of despondency, and take quantum leaps of faith in the Lord. Give us the spirit of conquest that Caleb had when he saw a huge mountain in front of him. He didn't tremble or recoil or doubt or fear. Something of the Lord God Almighty rose up inside of him, which is rising inside of us now, and he said, "Give me that mountain." As deep speaks unto deep, we speak one to another, to that well which is resident in every one of God's children—spring up, O well!

Lord, transform us from weak, murmuring, faltering, double-minded Christians into loving, consistent, credible, powerful warriors full of conquest. We want to be known as conquestors and conquerors, and, Lord, we ask You to take it up a notch. Just as the Scripture was just read, not only make us conquerors, but make us more than conquerors through Him Who loves us.

We want to be part of the solution, and not part of the problem. We want to be known as repairers of broken walls, restorers of streets with dwellings, and we ask You, Lord, in these momentous days, where You have just begun to pour out the latter rain of Your Spirit, to use us to rebuild ancient ruins and raise up age-old foundations. Give us the spiritual dunamis to dispossess the gates of the enemy, and possess the land, to take back which we have previously lost by default. We thank You, Lord, as we speak, there is a centrifuge of Your Spirit moving in such a manner that before this day is over, many will know that they have been visited by the living Lord Jesus Christ, and

> "Lord, transform us from weak, murmuring, faltering, double-minded Christians into loving, consistent, credible, powerful warriors full of conquest."

that God Almighty has intervened in human affairs in a supernatural way. Lord, help us to press these battles all the way to the gates. We are beseeching You this morning, not only for deliverance, but great deliverance, so much so, that when it happens, none of us will ever be the same. Some will feel so different. It's as if they have received a new name, and everyone who knows anything about us will realize that Jehovah Almighty has personally stepped into our situation to bring radical, unprecedented, monumental, breakthroughs. We celebrate You, again, this morning, Lord, as the God of the breakthroughs.

Regardless of what we think, You are never too late. Send battalions and regiments of swift, militant angels to move out on the wings of the wind and provide supernatural assistance, reinforcement, deliverance and provision. Inspire us to actually do what it says in Isaiah 52:2.

> **"Lord, help us to press these battles all the way to the gates."**

"Shake off your dust; rise up, sit enthroned, O Jerusalem. Free yourself from the chains on your neck, O captive Daughter of Zion."

Remove far from us any vestige of religion. God, spare Your people from the hectic, frenzied, fast-paced activity of empty, sterile, hollow religious activities. Impart to us an unprecedented disdain for anything religious. Let us be able to smell it a mile away and keep our distance. We hunger for that which has the depth and substance and fullness and fragrance of Your Spirit resident in it. We recoil backwards from that which is ecclesiastical and has the sound of tinkling cymbals and sounding brass. We pray that Your people would be able to distinguish between the two, and no longer tolerate such a travesty, such misrepresentation, such counterfeiting of the real thing. We realize if we were guilty of this kind of misrepresentation in the business world, we would be sued. We realize, Lord, that in Scripture, every time, without exception, that resurrection power was released to free a captive, or heal a sick person, or raise the dead, or cleanse a leper, or to release miracle-working power, or exhibit signs and wonders, every time, without exception, a religious spirit would raise up its ugly head in the form of a scribe or Pharisee or Sanhedrin, or teacher of the law, or high priest. They would be anointed from the other side and would demonically resist the anointing of Your Spirit.

> "We pray there would be such a demonstration of Your Spirit that the world system would be drawn to our gatherings. . . ."

Therefore, without hesitation or apology, we ask You, Lord, to expose every religious spirit in this country, whether it operates in a board of deacons, or pontificates from the pulpits of this city. Let them recoil backwards in abject horror and intrepidation. Let them gasp and be throttled down, and be driven into dry places to await the Judgment Day. In the place of this, Lord, we ask You to impart a fresh anointing, release miracle-working power into Your Church, emanate forth with the essence of Your

Spirit accompanied by a sweet fragrance from the Lord. Let not our church organizations any longer be listed in the Yellow Pages under Country Club. We pray there would be such a demonstration of Your Spirit that the world system would be drawn to our gatherings and we would once again witness deep, intense, piercing conviction which would cause peoples' hearts to melt and lives to be permanently, radically transformed. This is what it's all about. Do it, Lord. You've done it before in history. We believe You're preparing to do it again. Hasten the day.

In Jesus' name, amen.

Additional Scripture References

I Corinthians 15:58
Therefore, my dear brothers, stand firm. Let nothing move you. Always give yourselves fully to the work of the Lord, because you know that your labor in the Lord is not in vain.

Psalm 63:1, 2
O God, you are my God, earnestly I seek you; my soul thirsts for you, my body longs for you, in a dry and weary land where there is no water. I have seen you in the sanctuary and beheld your power and your glory.

Psalm 84:1, 2
How lovely is your dwelling place, O Lord Almighty! My soul yearns, even faints, for the courts of the Lord; my heart and my flesh cry out

for the living God.

Philippians 4:6, 7
Do not be anxious about anything, but in everything, by prayer and petition, with thanksgiving, present your requests to God. And the peace of God, which transcends all understanding, will guard your hearts and your minds in Christ Jesus.

Romans 8:37-39
No, in all these things we are more than conquerors through him who loved us. For I am convinced that neither death nor life, neither angels nor demons, neither the present nor the future, nor any powers, neither height nor depth, nor anything else in all creation, will be able to separate us from the love of God that is in Christ Jesus our Lord.

~15~

Prayer for Forgetting the Former Things

Dear Lord, we thank You that You do all things well. We praise You that regardless of what we have done in the last few hours or last few days, that as we ask forgiveness from You and others, You make us as white as snow, and You are our justification, and justification means, just as if we had never sinned. We celebrate such great salvation we enjoy in You this day. You are indeed a great Savior. Help those who are listening who are grappling with feelings of guilt and shame to realize that You forgive and forget. You cast our sins into the sea of forgetfulness. You place them as far as the East is from the West. There is no East Pole. There is no West Pole. There is no latitude. There is no longitude. There is no way to relocate them and there is no fishing in the sea of God's forgetfulness.

Some out there are having problems forgetting. They are haunted by the past. They are stumbling because they are going through life looking through the rearview mirror. They are full of regrets. They can't seem to shake it. It's a tormenting harassment of the enemy to play old tapes, bring up flashbacks, to entertain regrets, to mull over remorse. To continually say, "if only," or "what if?". Lord, in Jesus' name, we ask for a fresh anointing of Your Spirit right now, that will go deep into the core of their being and help them to do as Paul did, and it was obvious it was an urgent priority of his: *". . .one thing I do: Forgetting what is behind and straining toward what is ahead, I press on toward the goal to win the prize for which God has called me heavenward in Christ Jesus" (Philippians 3:13, 14).*

Help them to realize Your promise in Isaiah 42:9.

"See, the former things have taken place, and new things I declare; before they spring into being I announce them to you."

Also, we pray that You will personally confirm to them that despite how difficult it is, how rocky the road, how much the opposition, regardless of how intense the warfare, or how much it hurts, that what You say in Philippians 1:6 is true for them and that they will appropriate it for themselves, *"being confident of this, that he who began a good work in you will carry it on to completion until the day of Christ Jesus."* And the Scripture portion in Psalm 138:8, *"The Lord will fulfill his purpose for me; . . ."* And the one in Proverbs 4:18, *"The path of the righteous is like the first gleam of dawn, shining ever brighter till the full light of day."*

For those who are a little shaky this morning, who are uncertain about their future, they're traveling uncharted waters, they're facing difficult circumstances, help them to know this morning, as they trust You with all their heart, and rely not on their own resources or understanding, that You are a Sovereign God and You have everything under control. We pray that You will help stabilize them and be an anchor to their soul.

86

We thank You, Lord, You are such a Sovereign God. You are the Alpha and Omega. You know the end from the beginning, that You foil the plans of the heathen. You thwart the purposes of evil people and Your plans stand firm forever and the purposes of Your heart throughout all generations (Psalm 33:10, 11). You foil the signs of false prophets and make fools of diviners. You overthrow the learning of the wise and turn it into nonsense. You carry out the words of Your servants and fulfill the predictions of Your messengers. Encourage Your people this day that You are a Sovereign God and that indeed, You have everything under control.

> "For those who are a little shaky this morning, . . . We pray that You will stabilize them and be an anchor to their soul."

Now, for the disconsolate, the disheartened, the discouraged, the hurting, the wounded, the confused, the oppressed, let these eternal truths, this anointed rhema word be quickened to them. Let it make the Divine exchange in their life of a spirit of heaviness for garments of praise. Let these words from the Word minister to those who think they have crashed and burned and turn ashes into beauty. Come, Lord Jesus, let this eternal, unchanging, anointed Word do its office work this day and these children of Yours will never, ever be the same.

In the name of Jesus, amen.

Additional Scripture References

Psalm 9:9, 10
The Lord is a refuge for the oppressed, a stronghold in times of trouble. Those who know your name will trust in you, for you, Lord, have never forsaken those who seek you.

Deuteronomy 33:27
The eternal God is your refuge, and underneath are the everlasting arms. He will drive out your enemy before you, saying, 'Destroy him!'

Exodus 14:13, 14
Moses answered the people, "Do not be afraid. Stand firm and you will see the deliverance the Lord will bring you today. The Egyptians you see today you will never see again. The Lord will fight for you; you need only to be still."

Psalm 27:5, 6
For in the day of trouble he will keep me safe in his dwelling; he will hide me in the shelter of his tabernacle and set me high upon a rock. Then my head will be exalted above the enemies who surround me; at his tabernacle will I sacrifice with shouts of joy; I will sing and make music to the Lord.

~16~

Prayer for
Destiny and Purpose

Dear Lord, we pray that this prayer time would be the most productive, the most impactful few minutes of our day, and as a result of this small concert of prayer, we would experience significant changes before this day is over. We thank You, Lord, You didn't die to make us religious, but You died to radically change our lives. We thank You for life-transforming help which is available through our Lord Jesus Christ. We are especially burdened for those listening who have heard hundreds, and some, thousands of sermons, and are still grappling with some of the same basic enslavements, fixations, oppressions and compulsions that they have wrestled with for years. God have mercy. Show them that this thing called the Christian life really works and that the name of this whole thing is "change"—life-changing transformation by the living power of our Lord and Savior, Jesus Christ.

Help them to realize what it says in Second Corinthians 3:6, that the letter killeth, but the Spirit giveth life. And what Paul said in First Corinthians 4:20, that the kingdom of God is not a matter of talk but of power. And what he said in First Corinthians 1:17, *"For Christ. . ."* sent me to *"preach the gospel—not with words of human wisdom, lest the cross*

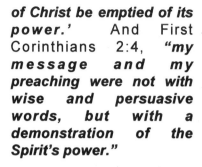

"Lord, we need more than sermons, outlines, notes, seminars, and therapy sessions."

of Christ be emptied of its power.' And First Corinthians 2:4, *"my message and my preaching were not with wise and persuasive words, but with a demonstration of the Spirit's power."*

Lord, we need more than sermons, outlines, notes, seminars and therapy sessions. We need a modern day demonstration of Your power that will leave us breathless, with our mouths wide open, awestruck, smitten, something that will indelibly impact our lives forever. And when the Gospel is preached, we pray that we would return back to New Testament norm and let the Word be confirmed with signs following.

Lord, forgive us for sitting around in our boring church services singing the first, second and last. Forgive us for having organized the awesome presence, anointing and power of the Holy Spirit out of our gatherings. We pray the heart cry of the Lord in Malachi 1:10, *"Oh, that one of you would shut the temple doors, so that you would not light useless fires on my altar! . . ."* We say amen to that Scripture and away with useless man-made fires. In the place of that, ignite us with the fire of God like that which fell on Elijah's water-logged offering at the contest between God and 450 prophets of Baal and 400 prophets of Ashterah.

We desperately need nothing less than a historically unprecedented spiritual visitation which will supersede anything we have read in history about the Early Awakening which impacted our entire nation and the Welsh revival. God, we personally invite You, at whatever the cost, to invade our lukewarm, sterile, powerless, unanointed, business-as-usual, perfunctory church gatherings and come with a life-transforming, breath of God, miracle-producing, fruit-bearing move of Your Holy Spirit. Our hearts are hungry. Help us to leave our comfort zone and pray like it says in Isaiah 62:6, 7.

"I have posted watchmen on your walls, O Jerusalem; they will never be silent day or night. You who call on the Lord, give yourselves no rest,

and give him no rest. . . ."

We believe there are people out there listening who are tired of the low life, the mediocre existence, just making it. They're in a deep rut and there is something working inside of their spirit that is urging them upward and onward, to leave the survival mentality and take the high road, whatever the cost, to burn their bridges behind them, put their hands to the plow and not look back, launch into the deep, and set their faces like flint, like Jesus did, and go for the gold that God has ordained in their lives. Lord, You have a plan for each of us from the foundation of the world. It has been inordinately opposed. And for this reason, many are experiencing deep inexplicable frustration.

Our enemy has tried to hinder it every way he can. But by Your grace, many this day are getting back on track and are sensing for the first time, in a long time, that they are people of destiny and a vital part of what You are currently doing in the kingdom. We ask You, Lord, this week, to reach deep down into the core of their being and motivate them to search after You as if they were seeking after silver and gold. Let them be like Jacob when he wrestled with the angel and would not let him go until the angel blessed him. Before this week is over, let them have one of the most dramatic breakthrough testimonies they have ever personally witnessed.

Do such a transforming work that things that used to enamor them, they lose interest in.   The things of this world that used to entice them no longer hold their interest. Spirits of seduction which used to prey upon them no longer have power over them. Let them be able to say as Jesus said, "satan comes, but he has nothing in Me." All of a sudden, they realize their entire life is being re-prioritized. They're doing a 180 and they're headed in a totally different direction. Make it real to them what Your Word says about not being conformed any longer to the pattern of this world, but give them a strong desire to be transformed by the renewing of their minds. Then You will smite confusion from their lives,

"Lord, You have a plan for each of us from the foundation of the world."

then things will become clear. Then they will be able to test and approve what God's will is—Your good, pleasing and perfect will.

We ask You, Lord, to come and preempt our agendas. We lay down our plans, our schedules, our life-goals and ask You to visit us as never before, speak indelibly to our hearts, and get us headed in Your direction.   If any have gotten off track, or been distracted, we pray they would repent of this. Lord, we give You permission right now to gently jerk the slack out of our lives, and let us no longer waste precious time. We are love slaves of the Lord Jesus Christ.

We pray that these Scriptures on seeking the Lord will gently explode in their faces, become rhema, and let it be so effectual that those listening will realize that unusual transformations are occurring in their lives, even as we speak.

"Those who know your name will trust in you, for you, Lord, have never forsaken those who seek you."

Psalm 9:10

"My heart says of you, 'Seek his face!' Your face, Lord, I will seek."

Psalm 27:8

"I sought the Lord, and he answered me; he delivered me from all my fears."

Psalm 34:4

"As the deer pants for streams of water, so my soul pants for you, O God.

My soul thirsts for God, for the living God. When can I go and meet with God?"

Psalm 42:1, 2

"My soul years, even faints, for the courts of the Lord; my heart and my flesh cry out for the living God."

Psalm 84:2

In the name of Jesus, amen.

93

~17~

Prayer for Healing

Dear Lord, today we pray for those who are terrorized concerning the report they have received concerning their physical well being, and for those who are being held hostage by the adversary because of serious symptoms that have sprung up in their bodies, that have alarmed them and gripped their hearts with icy fear. We pray that You would visit upon them. Remove every vestige of anxiety, panic and apprehension. Banish far from them the evil whisperings of the adversary.

Lord, there are those who are listening who really, really don't believe that You still heal, that You still do miracles, that You still do the supernatural. They have been told it's not for this dispensation and it passed away with the apostles. Have mercy upon the ministries who perpetrate such heresy and unbelief. They've been brainwashed by traditions of men. They've been duped by religion and been subject to strong disillusionment and doubt concerning the miracle-working power of the Lord. Help them to unlearn every religious thing, remove every ecclesiastical stumbling block, disregard doctrines of devils, take the sectarian blinders off their eyes, and give them a mindset of faith. Quicken Your Word to them. Let it dwell in them richly and introduce them to New Testament Church and New Testament healing virtue.

Etch into their hearts and minds that You are their personal physician and that healing is waiting in the wings. We claim this promise in Isaiah 53:4, 5.

"Surely he took up our infirmities and carried our sorrows, yet we considered him stricken by God, smitten by him, and afflicted.

But he was pierced for our transgressions, he was crushed for our iniquities; the punishment that brought us peace was upon him, and by his wounds we are healed."

We ask You, Lord, to go to the source cause. Let the axe be laid to the root. Bring revelation concerning any root problem You want to bring to light. If there is residual darkness from a previous relationship, be their great Deliverer.

> "Etch into their hearts and minds that You are their personal physician and that healing is waiting in the wings."

If the door was ever opened for any kind of evil, shut the door and rid them of it. If there is any kind of generational curse, Lord, You are faithful. You said that even though the sins of the fathers are visited upon the second, third, and fourth generation, Your blessings reach to a thousand generations and that's a classic example of how redemptive You are. Help us to think that redemptively about ourselves and others we are related to. Drive far from these dear people the evil terrorist who goes about like a roaring lion seeking whom he may devour. Cause worry and anxiety to melt away and let them, right now, by Your Spirit, experience the most incredible wave of peace descending upon them. Let it be like a cool breeze. Let it be the antithesis of the anxiety, worry, panic and frustration which has tormented them. Do it, Lord, in such a manner that would supersede anything they've ever experienced.

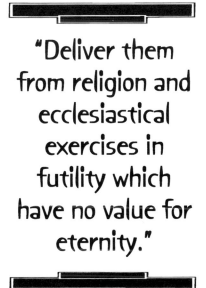

"Deliver them from religion and ecclesiastical exercises in futility which have no value for eternity."

We pray further for those who are suffering mental torment, regret, remorse, insomnia, anxiety, and paralyzing fear. First of all, let them know that they know that they are a born-again child of the living God. If there is any question, let them settle it right now. Give them the grace to repent, turn from their sinful way and receive You wholeheartedly as their own personal Savior. "If any man be in Christ, he is a new creature—old things pass away, and all things become new." Let this be their testimony. Then baptize them in the Holy Spirit. Then give them an insatiable hunger and thirst for You and Your Word and fellowship with God's people. Then place them in a loving, solid, balanced, anointed New Testament-type fellowship. Then deliver them from spirit forces of darkness that promote torment, and let them experience the incredible, inexplicable peace that passes all understanding. Descend upon them with this supernatural tranquility—even as we speak.

Visit upon them in a personal, intimate manner. Deliver them from religion and ecclesiastical exercises in futility which have no value for eternity. Give them the mind of Christ. We thank You for Your Word in Isaiah 26:3, 4.

"You will keep in perfect peace him whose mind is steadfast, because he trusts in you.

Trust in the Lord forever, for the Lord, the Lord, is the Rock eternal."

Also, this Scripture in Philippians 4:8.

"Finally, brothers, whatever is true, whatever is noble, whatever is right, whatever is pure, whatever is lovely, whatever is admirable—if anything is excellent or praiseworthy—think about such things."

We celebrate You again this day as our Great Physician, as our Rapha Healer, and the One Who already has accomplished what we need on Calvary. By Your wounds and by Your stripes we are already healed. We avail ourselves of this river of life today.

In Jesus' name, amen.

~18~

Prayer for
Dispelling Fear

Dear Lord, we pray that the next few moments would be some of the most impactful that we will experience this day because You are a living, sovereign God, and You are deeply concerned about the affairs of Your people, and You are the One Who comes to our rescue. We pray to You, Lord, right now, for those who desperately need You to intervene in their lives this day. You are a faithful God. In the power of agreement, we pray that You would show Yourself so strong to them, totally invade their lives, reveal Your right arm, and press this battle to the gates. Lord, we appeal to You, because time is of the essence, and You are never late.

We thank You that the angel of the Lord encamps about those who fear You. We pray to You, God of all comfort, to dispatch numerous angels into their jurisdiction, take up their post, guard over, minister to, and wage war for those of Your children who feel at this moment like they are drowning.

You are the One Who told us to speak to this mountain and it too shall be removed. You are the One Who fights our battles. You are our defender, our vindicator, our representative, our attorney, our spokesman. You are the One Who sticks closer than a brother. To the widows, You are their husband, a close intimate friend. To the orphans, You are their Father. To the businessmen, You are the One Who can so radically turn things through prayer in such a short period of time that they will end up, as it says in Deuteronomy 28, lending and not borrowing. You are the One that can so radically turn the tables on darkness and so dramatically invade our lives, and so thoroughly alter our circumstances, that we will end up being the head and not the tail, above only and not below.

We pray for the disconsolate, the downcast, those not soon comforted, the oppressed, the despairing, those who have had a dark, foreboding cloud of gloom descend upon their lives, darkness so thick that you can nearly touch it. Be the Lily of their Valley, the Bright and Morning Star. Bring the anointing spoken of in Isaiah 61 that comforts all who mourn, provides for those who grieve in Zion, bestows on them a crown of beauty instead of ashes, the oil of gladness instead of mourning and a garment of praise instead of a spirit of despair.

> "You are the One that can so radically turn the tables on darkness and so dramatically invade our lives. . .that we will end up being the head and not the tail. . . ."

Lord, we humble ourselves and acknowledge that when we have run out of options, when we have expended all of our own human resources, when we are desperate, when we have nowhere to turn but to You, You are our very life; You are the breath that we breathe; You are our oxygen line. You are the One Who has the answer when we have run out of answers; You are the God of the impossible; You are well able, whether by few or many. You are the One Who can suddenly burst on the scene of our lives and bring radical changes. You are the One Who opens doors where there are no doors. One of Your names in Scriptures is "the Door." You make a way where there is no way. Come this morning and be our Waymaker.

We pray this morning that everyone hearing this prayer, before this day is over, would be lifted out of their slough of despondency, that You would come and break the evil yoke, put to flight the heavy oppression, and visit upon Your children with Your awesome presence, love and power. Before the midnight hour, let them know there is a God in Israel, there is a God in the United States of America, there is a God in Atlanta, and there is a God that intervenes in the affairs of men and in their personal lives, Who hasn't forgotten their address, Who cares intensely about every minute detail of their lives. Lord, bring them from dead religion into an intimate, personal, awesome relationship with their living Lord, Jesus Christ.

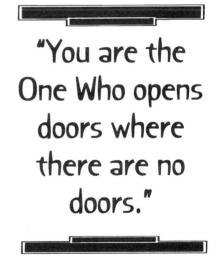

"You are the One Who opens doors where there are no doors."

Right now, by faith, we cast every burden, every deadline,

financial responsibility, and loved one on You. You are our burden bearer. Remove the iron yoke from our shoulders, and at the same time, we take Your yoke, Your burden. It's easy, it's light, and it brings rest to our souls.

We pray Your Word in Isaiah 52:1, 2.

"Awake, awake, O Zion, clothe yourself with strength. Put on your garments of splendor, O Jerusalem, the holy City. The uncircumcised and defiled will not enter you again.

Shake off your dust; rise up, sit enthroned, O Jerusalem. Free yourself from the chains on your neck, O captive Daughter of Zion."

We ask You, Prince of Peace, to personally visit Your people, calm shattered nerves, soothe jittery stomachs. Pour the oil of Your Spirit on them. Give them Your grace to relieve their pressure, tension, and restlessness, and fears, and bring them into a place of peace and tranquility. Restore back to them the joy of Your salvation so they can teach transgressors Your ways. Let the Prince of Peace rule and reign over our lives once again.

We thank You for Your promise that You will keep those in perfect peace whose minds are fastened upon You. We thank You for Your promise that we are not to be conformed to this world system, but to be transformed by the renewing of our minds. Right now, we pull down every stronghold and everything that exalts itself above the knowledge of God. By the precious Blood of Jesus Christ and the washing of the Word, renew our minds. Give us Your thoughts that flow directly from Your heart. Give us the mind of Christ. By Your grace, we shall no longer mull over things that are depressing and heavy and burdensome that minister fear and panic, but we shall think on things that are true, noble, right, pure, lovely, admirable. If anything is excellent or praiseworthy, help us to fix our mind on these things. Let the Word of Christ dwell in us richly.

We speak to smothering spirits of infirmity who have been running roughshod over the saints. How dare you! You will not deface God's property. You will not arrogantly stand up against the living God. For those who feel like they are prisoners of their pain-wracked bodies, we call upon the healing virtue of the Lord Jesus Christ, our

"Lord, transform us from murmurers to worshippers."

Rapha Healer, the Great Physician. We call upon that same power that raised Christ Jesus from the dead. We call upon our all powerful Lord who is the same yesterday, today, and forever. Lord, if You did it in the days of old, if You did it in the New Testament, if You did it in the book of Acts, You can do it today. You are a consistent God. Meet these dear people just where they are this morning, right now, and let them experience a gentle surging of Your Spirit, wave after wave of the same power that raised Christ Jesus from the dead.

Lord, help us, as it says in Isaiah 43:18, 19, to

"Forget the former things; do not dwell on the past.

See, I am doing a new thing! Now it springs up; do you not perceive it? I am making a way in the desert and streams in the wasteland."

Lord, transform us from murmurers to worshippers. Grant that we would never be like the nine lepers, who were healed of a terminal disease, and arrogantly, presumptuously went on their merry way without a word of thanksgiving. But Lord, help us by Your grace to be like the one leper who turned back, and with tears of gratitude, lavishly and profusely worshipped at Your feet for such an incredible manifestation of God's healing power and love.

Lord, we acknowledge that You are the preeminent One. You are all-powerful. You are omnipotent. You are omniscient. You are omnipresent. There is none other. There is no other God like You. You are superior to every other principality and power and potentate. This day we celebrate Your Lordship over every area of our lives.

In the name of Jesus, we pray. Amen.

Additional Scripture References

1 Corinthians 13:4-7

Isaiah 40:9, 10

Psalm 23:2

Exodus 33:14

Psalm 4:8

Psalm 116:7

Matthew 11:29

Romans 8:6

Romans 14:17

Psalm 119:165

Isaiah 26:3

John 14:27

Philippians 4:7

Romans 5:1

Colossians 3:15

Job 22:21

Isaiah 43:1-3

~19~

Prayer for Trusting God

Dear Lord, as we stand on the threshold of this new week and a new month, we ask You to do a new thing in response to the prayers of Your people. Come and upset the status quo. Move mountains. Lift people out of ruts. Let things be different. Let it not be business as usual. Break through stalemates. Let the awesome Shekinah Glory of God come down upon us. We are hungry for more of You. We are thirsty for You. As it says in Psalm 63:1

"O God, you are my God, earnestly I seek you; my soul thirsts for you, my body longs for you, in a dry and weary land where there is no water."

Lord, we are no longer satisfied with typical, business as usual, conventional religious meetings where people sit around and perfunctorily sing the first, second and last. That day is over. We want to hear an anointed rhema word from You. Lord, we want to minister to You. We want to go from praise to high praise to worship to high worship and warfare worship. We desire for the electric presence of the living God to invade our gatherings and impact lives where people are never the same and the results are life-changing.

Let the way be clear. Let nothing stand in the way. We pray that we will be up-to-date with You and each other. By the grace of God, let Your people keep short accounts. Let it not be said of any that they were turned over to the tormentors because they were forgiven so much and didn't, in comparison, forgive so little. We acknowledge that we cannot afford the luxury of harboring resentment, bitterness, unforgiveness. Right now, we mentally tear up all of our IOU's. Just like John the Baptist prepared the way of the Lord, so we, right now, prepare the way for the Lord to come four-square upon Christians in this area.

Let every high thing, every arrogant thing come down. Let every valley, every oppressed thing be lifted up. Let the crooked ways be made straight and the rough plains be made smooth. Let the way be totally prepared so the Lord can visit us this week as never before. We pray that testimonies will come in that this indeed has been a breakthrough time for many of God's people. Let faith loom large in our hearts. Replace hopelessness with a measure of hope that has exceeded anything we have ever experienced. Replace despair, gloom, a heavy foreboding cloud, with the joy of the Lord, which is our strength, and an electric expectancy and joyful expectation concerning what You're preparing to do.

We decree that this will, by the grace of God, and through the power of prayer be a week that will go down in our memory bank as a pivotal, significant, monumental week. For those whose perspective about their future has been warped, give them vision—Your vision. Clear the cobwebs and confusion out of their minds. Bring clarity. The children of God are led by the Spirit of God. Give them spiritual eyes to see more than just what they see in the natural. Give them

Your outlook on life and let them know that their future is as bright as the promises of God, and their best days lie yet ahead. By Your Spirit, pull the curtain back a little more to help them to have revelation of what the Spirit of the Lord is doing in this day.

Help them to know personally what it says in Isaiah 60, that even though darkness covers the earth,

"For those whose perspective about their future has been warped, give them vision— Your vision."

and gross darkness the people, the light is arising upon them. In agreement with intercessors all over Atlanta, we pray that the brilliant splendor of Your light will pierce through all darkness. We pray that such a volume of prayer will mount up in Your Church that the heyday of wickedness will be over, and this area will no longer be conducive for the subtle, crafty, insidious works of darkness, but we will witness the tide turning, and the very environment will be conducive for righteousness and a spiritual awakening will break out in Marietta and Atlanta.

For those who are suffering depression, break off of these people a heavy, dark, foreboding cloud and we pray for them Your Word in Psalm 51:12, 13.

"Restore to me the joy of your salvation and grant me a willing spirit, to sustain me.

Then I will teach transgressors your ways, and sinners will turn back to you."

Let the joy of the Lord be their strength. Converge on them, dear Lord, suddenly, meet them right where they are and be the lifter of their heads. And instead of entertaining self-pity and licking their wounds and feeling sorry for themselves, all of a sudden, they will find themselves being restored, the joy of the Lord being their strength, and they will begin to minister to the Lord and reach out to others and teach transgressors Your ways. By the Spirit, they will go from being introverted to extroverted. Do it today, Lord. It will be revolutionary. We ask You, Lord, to invade our lives, change our minds, adjust our attitudes, alter our directions, rearrange our priorities. We invite You, Lord Jesus, to preempt our schedules. Clean house. We are totally at Your disposal. We submit every arena of our lives to the Lordship of Jesus Christ. Come with Your living, anointed, vibrant presence. Come, rend the heavens, descend as a Heavenly Dove. We invite You. Come down and visit Your people. Let this week and this month be known as a time of unprecedented visitation.

We thank You, Lord, that everything that has to do with You flows forward, not backward. We thank You for Your Word that promises that as we trust You, You will take us from one degree of grace to another, one degree of glory to another, and one degree of strength to another. For those who are weak, as they wait upon You, just as Scripture promises, let them mount up with wings as eagles. Let them run and not be weary and walk and not faint. There is power in the Blood of Jesus Christ. We lay solid claim to Your Word that by Your stripes, we are already healed.

Help us to receive Your challenge this day to be men and women of prayer and the Word and men and women of faith. As a matter of fact, let that be our greatest ambition in life—to fulfill Your total calling for us and never to make peace with

110

mediocrity. As it was said of the Lord Jesus Christ, let the zeal of the Lord of hosts accomplish all of this.

Remove from us, dear Lord, ignorance and naivete of what You are doing in our day. Take off the blinders. Give us the wisdom and anointing that the children of Issachar had who not only had a sense of the Lord's agenda, and what He was doing, what season they were in, but also knew what to do in that season. Lord, give us that excellence of wisdom. Help us not to be like those in Luke 19 who did not recognize the day of Your visitation. We pray that just like the children of Israel, when the cloud begins to move, so we will be responsive and move with it. Help us to not conform any longer to the pattern of this world, but be transformed by the renewing

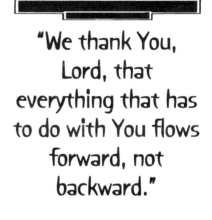

"We thank You, Lord, that everything that has to do with You flows forward, not backward."

of our minds so that we can be able to test and approve what God's will is—Your good, pleasing and perfect will.

Help us to seek after You as if we were seeking for silver or gold. We thank You for Your Word in Psalm 19:9-11.

"The fear of the Lord is pure, enduring forever. The ordinances of the Lord are sure and altogether righteous.

They are more precious than gold, than much pure gold; they are sweeter than honey, than honey from the comb.

By them is your servant warned; in keeping them there is great

reward."

We thank You that Your Word hones our discernment and by Your Word we are warned. Thank You for Your protection, Your watchcare. Thank You, Lord, that You came not only to bring life, but to bring it more abundantly.

In Jesus' name, amen.

Additional Scripture References

Deuteronomy 31:6, 8
Isaiah 41:10, 13
Matthew 11:28-30

~20~

Prayer for Knowing the High Calling of God in Our Lives

Dear Lord, this morning we desire to do kingdom business with You. We thank You for Your promise that if we call unto You, You would answer us and show us great and unsearchable things we do not know. We thank You, Lord, that when we cry to You that You answer us from Your holy hill (Psalm 3:4).

Psalm 9:10
"Those who know your name will trust in you, for you, Lord, have never forsaken those who seek you."

Just as Your Word does not return void but accomplishes that for which You sent it, so, we pray that every word that we ever utter in prayer will reflect the Father's heart, will actually be the Lord's prayer for this moment and hit its target.

We thank You, Lord, that every conquest, every manifest victory that we experienced this year was purely because of Your grace. As is stated in Psalm 44:3,

"It was not by their sword that they won the land, nor did their arm bring them victory; it was your right hand, your arm, and the light of your face, for you loved them."

Psalm 68:9, 10
"You gave abundant showers, O God; you refreshed your weary inheritance.

Your people settled in it, and from your bounty, O God, you provided for the poor."

Lord, we repent and ask forgiveness for our rebellion, prayerlessness and idolatry. Restore true spiritual authority to the Church in Atlanta so that once again, we would experience the exponential increase of power the way it was initially planned so that one of us would put to flight a thousand of the enemy, two ten thousand, three a hundred thousand, four a million and seven a billion so that every time a brother or sister agrees with us in prayer the decimal is moved over one. Lord, give us this kind of "decimal, decimating" power. Raise up these kind of intercessors and prayer groups in Atlanta. Thank You, Lord, for being the Lamb of God and the Lion of Judah. This is the day the Lord has made. We shall rejoice and be glad in it.

As we approach the closing of this season, and are not too far from a brand new year, our hearts are overwhelmed with Your blessings of the past year. You are a generous benefactor. Your mercies are new every morning. You daily load us with benefits. For those who fear You, You have promised they will lack nothing. Let this be real, right now, in the lives of those listening and who feel there is a large, substantial lack, an aching sense of emptiness or unfulfillment, or gaping hole in their lives. Whether it be financial or relational, let this Word be quickened to them from Psalm

34:9, 10.

"Fear the Lord, you his saints, for those who fear him lack nothing.

The lions may grow weak and hungry, but those who seek the Lord lack no good thing."

We pray these promises in Psalms, Isaiah and Jeremiah for those who are feeling empty, unfulfilled and incomplete. The Lord satisfies Your desires with good things so that Your youth is renewed like the eagle's (Psalm 103:5).

"The Lord will guide you always; he will satisfy your needs in a sun-scorched land and will strengthen your frame. You will be like a well-watered garden, like a spring whose waters never fail."

Isaiah 58:11

"'I will satisfy the priests with abundance, and my people will be filled with my bounty,' declares the Lord."

Jeremiah 31:14

"You will show me the path of life; in Your presence is fullness of joy, at Your right hand there are pleasures forevermore."

Psalm 16:11 (Amplified)

We pray Ephesians 3:19 that they would know God's love that surpasses knowledge, and that they would be filled to the measure of all the fullness of God. Help them to realize that in Christ all the fullness of the Deity lives in bodily form. Help them to experience Your fullness.

Motivate us, Your children, to delight ourselves in You, and as we do, You said You would give us the desires of our heart.

There are some out there who are trying to get their own desires without delighting themselves in You. Give us a renewed, increased hunger to seek Your face, to have night seasons with You, to initiate a quest to diligently pursue You as never before. During these busy days, we pray for businessmen out there who are extremely disciplined and enterprising to pursue and capture new business to be just as diligent and disciplined in seeking You as if they are seeking silver and gold. Help them to realize that as they seek first the kingdom of God and Your righteousness, all these other things will be added unto them. Let it be their burning desire and ambition to be as much or more of a Godly husband and father as they are an astute businessman. Motivate them to be as diligent in the things of the Spirit as they are in the pursuit for security and wealth, and to realize that real security is in Jesus Christ.

"Motivate us, Your children, to delight ourselves in You, and as we do, You said You would give us the desires of our heart."

Turn those who are listening from flighty, trivial, shallow, empty humans into anointed vessels of substance and depth, and elevate us back to the position of being honorable and stately and majestic and loving and powerful because these are Your attributes You want to impart to us as we seek You with all our heart.

Help Your people to realize that in Your presence is fullness of joy and at Your right hand are pleasures

116

forevermore. Show them, that in comparison, the pleasures and playthings of this world are but a hollow phantom shadow in contrast to the deep, lasting fulfillment and substance You have to offer. Let it be a Holy season, a powerful family time, a time of healing and restoration, one in which hearts are warmed, the Spirit of the Lord hovers over our households, and our hearts are drawn to You as never before.

Lord, we ask You to move so sovereignly in the lives of those listening, that testimonies will come in that indeed this has been a week in which significant, monumental changes have taken place in the lives of Your people in this city. For those who are mired down in circumstances and problems which have no human answer and feel they are on a dead-end road, we pray that they will totally yield themselves and every area of their lives to You. We celebrate You this day as the God of the breakthrough. We celebrate You as the above and beyond God. You are well able to do exceedingly abundantly above all that we ask or think. Lord, You are well able, by many or by few is of no consequence to You. We speak to the mountains in these peoples lives to be removed in Jesus' name.

Thank You for Your Word in Isaiah 42:16.

"I will lead the blind by ways they have not known, along unfamiliar paths I will guide them; I will turn the darkness into light before them and make the rough places smooth. These are the things I will do; I will not forsake them."

We pray that right now for those listening, there will be such a rich anointing, such a personal visitation of Your Spirit that they would experience, firsthand, Your leading those who feel they are spiritually blind by ways they have not known, along unfamiliar paths, You would guide them, turn their darkness into light right before them, and make the rough places smooth. Lord, You are the only One Who can take these tangled up, humanly impossible, gone-too-far situations, and supernaturally unravel them, melt them down in front of their eyes, bring resolution, restore, and make the rough places smooth. Show Yourself strong to them. Reveal Your right arm. Rend the heavens and come down this day. Do it now, we pray, by Your Spirit, in Jesus' name.

We thank You, Lord, that according to Your Word, we not only have a calling on our lives, not only a Holy calling, but a high and Holy calling which You have ordained for us from before the foundations of the earth. You have for everyone listening nothing less than a destiny of magnificence and we claim the Scripture in Jeremiah which states that it's a future which is full of hope and will not be cut off.

For those who are weary, on the threshold of burnout, because, indeed, they have left the way and calling and purpose of their God, we pray that they would not only be restored to the right path, but Lord, send them a season of refreshing. For those who need this kind of visitation, Lord, Your Word says, that if we would just turn and repent from our own ways, that You would indeed send a brand new season of refreshing, so that these will not be days that they just endure and suffer through, but be the most glorious holiday season of their entire lives. Send the wind of Your Spirit to grace their lives, right now, in Jesus' name.

Thank You, Lord, You indeed are the God of the new beginning. Thank You, Lord, for the anointing which binds up the brokenhearted, proclaims freedom for captives, release from darkness for the prisoners, comforts all who mourn, provides for those who grieve, and bestows on them a crown of beauty instead of ashes, the oil of gladness instead of mourning, and a garment of praise instead of a spirit of despair.

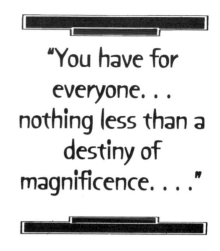

"You have for everyone. . . nothing less than a destiny of magnificence. . . ."

Lord, You are the Waymaker. You promised to be our guide till death. We intercede for those who have been subject to seducing and enticing spirits, who have listened to counterfeit voices, who have been drawn aside from their primary purpose in the Lord. They may have gotten off track a long time ago, but by Your grace, they can return into Your purposes just as quickly as they got off.

We ask You, right now, to cut through the confusion, the smokescreens, the decoys, the soulish counsel, the deception, counsel from false friends, and this week, get them back on track. Help them to tune out every other voice, as logical as it may seem, and listen diligently for the voice of the Lord. Help them, once more, to seek Your face in the Word of the living God. Help them to be lovers of God more than lovers of pleasure.

We declare that this week for many will be a week of getting back on track, turning back to the Bible, getting back into fellowship with You, and forsaking the ways of the world. Help them not to be conformed to this world system, but rather be transformed by the renewing of their minds, so they can know the good, pleasing and perfect will of God. We pray that this week would go down in history as one in which, by the grace of God, many of Your children find their way, and the

119

calling and purpose of God restored clearly back to them. We celebrate You as the God of the new beginning.

We claim Your Word in Isaiah 44:3-5.

"For I will pour water on the thirsty land, and streams on the dry ground; I will pour out my Spirit on your offspring, and my blessing on your descendants.

They will spring up like grass in a meadow, like poplar trees by flowing streams.

One will say, 'I belong to the Lord'; another will call himself by the name of Jacob; still another will write on his hand, 'The Lord's,' and will take the name Israel."

In Jesus' name, we pray. Amen.

Additional Scripture References

2 Samuel 22:29

Psalm 32:8

Psalm 48:14

Psalm 61:2

Psalm 73:24

Psalm 78:52

~21~

Prayer for
the Power of Prayer Agreement

Dear Lord, we are corporately standing in effectual prayer this morning for those Christians who have run into a brick wall, have met a major impasse, don't know where to turn, are feeling panicky and desperate, and need to have You intervene on their behalf—soon. We stand in the gap for them this morning.

For those who have totally run out of options, expended all of their resources, pursued a number of dead-end roads and are candidates for a breakthrough, we pray that the spiritual firepower generated by the few intercessors who are listening and are in agreement will be enough, this day, to cause that great reservoir in heaven, spoken of in Revelation 8, which holds the prayers of the saints, mixed with incense, on the golden altar before the throne, the smoke of which goes up before God—Lord, we pray that just like it is spoken of in Revelation 8, that You would cause the angel to take the censer, filled with fire from the altar, and hurl it on earth and that on behalf of those who are desperately waiting for You there would be peals of thunder, rumblings, flashes of lightning and an earthquake. As a result of our fervent

"Open the eyes of Your people to realize the incredible, incalculable, under-estimated power of prayer agreement. . . ."

prayers, let there be a shift in the heavenlies. Let the answer come, the way would be made, the door be open, the provision all of a sudden would be there, and their prayers for which they have labored for a long period of time would be answered.

Open the eyes of Your people to realize the incredible, incalculable, underestimated power of prayer agreement and give them the perseverance to press upward in prayer, until the answer comes. In Jesus' name, don't give up. Don't faint. The Word says in Luke 18 that we should always pray and not give up. Don't give up. Whatever you do, don't give up. The Lord's going to help you today to not become weary in well doing. You shall reap if you faint not. Don't lapse into a state of hopelessness. Don't entertain thoughts of despair. The Lord is coming. His awesome presence, through prayer, is being ushered into your vehicle, your home, hospital room, prison cell, business, wherever you are, He is omnipresent and His Sovereign presence is descending upon you as we speak.

We pray, this morning, that for those who are in need and desperate, that this ring of prayer warriors who are activated, right now, via radio waves, would be for them Aarons and Hurs to hold their hands up, just like they did for Moses when he was weak, weary and faint, and as they did, and as we do, the battle will be reversed on the battlefield, and they are going to stand by and watch the salvation of God. We pray also that the enemy they have grappled with, that has been a thorn in their flesh and vexed them 24 hours a day, stalked their path, been a fierce predator, made their way miserable, and taken their chariot wheels off, that enemy, from this day on, they would see no more.

Give these dear saints the grace and anointing, as it is stated in Ephesians 6, after having done all they can do, to stand. It's an honor for us corporately to bind and gag the powers of darkness which presents itself in doubt, unbelief, despair, hopelessness, discouragement, disillusionment, disease, depression. According to Psalm 149, it's an honor to exercise this authority and witness demon spirits gasp, and pant, and crash and burn as we crust satan under our feet.

And we do that right now. We speak Psalm 149 to the principalities and powers. Be subject to the Word of the living God.

"Let the saints rejoice in this honor and sing for joy on their beds.

May the praise of God be in their mouths and a double-edged sword in their hands,

to inflict vengeance on the nations and punishment on the peoples,

to bind their kings with fetters, their nobles with shackles of iron,

to carry out the sentence written against them. This is the glory of all his saints. . . ."

Psalm 149:5-9

Lord, we are laying claim to that Scripture in Isaiah 42 where You promised to lead the blind by ways they have not known, along unfamiliar paths. We thank You for that because we've never been this way before. You promised to turn our darkness into light before us, and make the rough places smooth. These are the things You said You would do and not forsake us. For this we are eternally grateful. We will praise You morning, noon and night. This is the day the Lord has made. We will be glad and rejoice in it. The latter part of this day is going to be far different than the former.

"The poor and needy search for water, but there is none; their tongues are parched with thirst. But I the Lord will answer them; I, the God of Israel, will not forsake them."

Isaiah 41:17

"How priceless if your unfailing love! Both high and low among men find refuge in the shadow of your wings.

They feast on the abundance of your house; you give them drink from your river of delights.

For with you is the fountain of life; in your light we see light."

Psalm 36:7-9

"Save me, O God, for the waters have come up to my neck.

I sink in the miry depths, where there is no foothold. I have come into the deep waters; the floods engulf me.

But I pray to you, O Lord, in the time of your favor; in your great love, O God, answer me with your sure salvation."

Psalm 69:1, 2; 13

We speak this Word right into the face of the enemy himself who is haranguing and tormenting Your people about the days to come.

"'For I know the plans I have for you,' declares the Lord, 'plans to prosper you and not to harm you, plans to give you hope and a future.

Then you will call upon me and come and pray to me, and I will listen to you.

You will seek me and find me when you seek me with all your heart.'"

Jeremiah 29:11-13

Lift Your people out of the slough of despondency. Shake them to the core of their being. Awaken them to the incredible potential they have in the Lord, and breathe upon them a fresh breath of God. Be an oxygen line to them while they are under stress to minister Divine CPR and rejuvenate them. Let them know of a surety today that if any man be in Christ, he is a new creature. Old things are passed away and all things become new.

In Jesus' name, amen.

Additional Scripture References

Isaiah 42:16
I will lead the blind by ways they have not known, along unfamiliar paths I will guide them; I will turn the darkness into light before them and make the rough places smooth. These are the things I will do; I will not forsake them.

Psalm 9:9
The Lord is a refuge for the oppressed, a stronghold in times of trouble.

Psalm 12:5
"Because of the oppression of the weak and the groaning of the needy, I will now arise," says the Lord. "I will protect them from those who malign them."

Psalm 40:1-3
I waited patiently for the Lord; he turned to me and heard my cry. He lifted me out of the slimy pit, out of the mud and mire; he set my feet on a rock and gave me a firm place to stand. He put a new song in my mouth, a hymn of praise to our God. Many will see and fear and put their trust in the Lord.

Isaiah 41:17
"The poor and needy search for water, but there is none; their tongues are parched with thirst. But I the Lord will answer them; I, the God of Israel, will not forsake them."

~22~

Prayer for Your Children

Dear Lord, this morning we are standing in the gap for our children, the youth of our city and nation, many of whom are preparing to leave the dungeons of darkness and be swept into the kingdom of God.

So that we can pray effectual prayers that avail much, we want to be up-to-date with You and each other and ask You, Lord, to search our hearts. See if there be any wicked way, forgive us, and cleanse us by the Blood of Jesus.

We intercede for parents who are despairing of their children, who are watching them go deeper into the dungeons of darkness, and drink at the cesspools of this world system, children who have naively been subject to spirits of seduction and enticement, been deceived, and have been siphoned into the spirit of this age. We ask You, Lord, to open parents' eyes and understanding to the reality of prayer—persistent, persevering prayer. Etch into their hearts what You say in Matthew 7:7, 8.

"'Ask and it will be given to you; seek and you will find; knock and the door will be opened to you.

For everyone who asks receives; he who seeks finds; and to him who knocks, the door will be opened.'"

We ask You, Lord, to quicken to parents, concerning the prayers for their children, what Your Word states in Jeremiah 33:3.

"'Call to me and I will answer you and tell you great and unsearchable things you do not know.'"

Also, fill them with joyful anticipation.

Concerning First Corinthians 2:9, **". . .No eye has seen, no ear has heard, no mind has conceived what God has prepared for those who love him"——.**

We claim Psalm 127:3-5.

"Sons are a heritage from the Lord, children a reward from him.

Like arrows in the hands of a warrior are sons born in one's youth.

Blessed is the man whose quiver is full of them. They will not be put to shame when they contend with their enemies in the gate."

We thank You for our children. They are a heritage from the Lord—a reward from You. Help everyone listening to perceive them as such, not as nuisances, but as gifts from God. They're like arrows in our hands. Give special grace to parents as they pull back the bow, little by little, and the pressure increases, but the day will come in which they will release that bow and their children will be sent straight to their target. Then the pressure will have been worth it all.

We acknowledge, Lord, according to Your Word, that You are raising up a young generation which will become movers and shakers in our society, who will be so fervent in the Lord, so bold, take such a stand, and move with such an anointing, that what Your Word says in Psalm 127:5 will come to pass. *". . .They will not be put to shame when they contend with their enemies in the gate."*

> "We acknowledge, Lord, according to Your Word, that You are raising up a young generation which will become movers and shakers in our society, . . ."

Therefore, regardless of what they look like now, or what diabolical thing they're caught up in, we are going to pray and take hold of the horns of the altar and stand in the gap and make up the hedge for our children until their testimony reads like Psalm 40:1-3.

"I waited patiently for the Lord; he turned to me and heard my cry.

He lifted me out of the slimy pit, out of the mud and mire; he set my feet on a rock and gave me a firm place to stand.

He put a new song in my mouth, a hymn of praise to our God. Many will see and fear and put their trust in the Lord."

We thank You, Lord, as we pray, You are going to turn the tables on satan himself. As we pray, he will go too far, he will overplay his hand, and our kids will actually become tired of sin, they'll get fed up with drugs, they'll realize the kicks have their kickbacks, and that sin has a price tag—the wages of sin

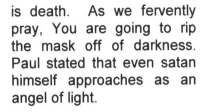

"Thank You, Lord, that as we pray, You are exposing the enemy of our children."

is death. As we fervently pray, You are going to rip the mask off of darkness. Paul stated that even satan himself approaches as an angel of light.

Therefore, Lord, we are going to pray that You remove the camouflage, and instead of our young people being seduced, snared and subtly drawn into demonic things which are made to appear so beautiful, appealing, and enticing, and being deceived, we are going to pray until You expose the other side for exactly what it is. Children will see it at face value, and instead of satan coming on to our kids in such a beautiful, alluring manner, our young people will be in abject shock. Because of the prayers of their parents, as they see exposed with their own eyes the venom and the fangs and the poison, they will recoil backwards as they smell the stench and see the putrefaction which the evil one has to offer.

Thank You, Lord, that as we pray, You are exposing the enemy of our children. Then You are going to draw them to the love and beauty of the Lord Jesus Christ. We are right now claiming a great harvest of youth all over this city.

Give parents vision to not just see them as they appear now, but what they're going to be when You arrest them in their tracks, grip their hearts, bring strong conviction, change their appetites, and redirect their lives. We are claiming household salvation, spoken of in Acts 16, for every family member that is being claimed this day.

Thank You, Lord, for hearing our prayer for our children. In Jesus' name we pray. Amen.

Additional Scripture References

Isaiah 49:16-18
"See, I have engraved you on the palms of my hands; your walls are ever before me. Your sons hasten back, and those who laid you waste depart from you. Lift up your eyes and look around; all your sons gather and come to you. As surely as I live," declares the Lord, "you will wear them all as ornaments; you will put them on, like a bride."

Jeremiah 31:15-17
This is what the Lord says: "A voice is heard in Ramah, mourning and great weeping, Rachel weeping for her children and refusing to be comforted, because her children are no more." This is what the Lord says: "Restrain your voice from weeping and your eyes from tears, for your work will be rewarded," declares the Lord. "They will return from the land of the enemy. So there is hope for your future," declares the Lord. "Your children will return to their own land."

~23~

Prayer For Our Families

Lord, we sense an Esther anointing this morning, that You have brought us into this place at such a strategic hour as this with an intercessory mantle on our heads, to stand in the gap, make up the hedge, to weep between the altar and the porch, and travail for a revival in the homes of America. You have given us the ministry of reconciliation, and through prayer we humbly exercise it this morning.

We thank You, Lord, that we are living in a day in which You are pouring out Your Spirit on all flesh. As You have momentarily turned us into an executive body to send forth decrees into the heavenlies through prayer, we ask You to move sovereignly and swiftly, and let the powerful, refreshing wind of Your Spirit sweep through the families of Atlanta. Lord, we desperately need our houses to be turned into homes.

Help us to identify with Your heartbeat as You sit on the brow of the hill of Atlanta, weeping over this city, calling it to Yourself just like a mother hen, so that our homes and our city will not be desolate. Show us how to intercede for this world-class city. Give us the capacity to weep tears of intercession for our homes.

We ask You, Lord, to turn the hearts of the fathers to the children and the hearts of the children to the fathers so the curse can be lifted off this land. Heal our marriages. Restore our families and the years where the cankerworm, palmer worm, locust and caterpillar have eaten.

We pray that just as smoke flees before the wind and as wax melts before the fire, so You, Lord God, would arise and the enemy be scattered. We ask You to clean house. We pray a "Jeremiah" anointing over our homes to root out, tear down, pluck out and destroy everything that is not of You so that You can plant and build that which is of You.

"We pray such a manifest presence of the Lord that when saint or sinner walks over our threshold, they would inhale Your savor."

Drive out the desert beasts, the screech owls, the hyenas, things that mutter and peep, and creep and crawl from our dwelling places. Remove the raw sewage from our living rooms. We ask You, Lord Jesus, to purge, cleanse and purify our homes by the washing of the Word and the Blood of Jesus Christ to the extent that it would be conducive for health and healing. Let the sound of rejoicing, once again, be heard in our tents. Let our homes be habitable places where springs of living water constantly flow. Lord, see fit to tabernacle amongst us.

We pray such a Godly environment of the Lord into our homes, that if we happened to awaken in the middle of the

134

night, it would be as if we could hear the rustling of Your garments moving through every room from the attic to the basement. Let the Prince of Peace rule and reign. Turn our homes into citadels of righteousness. We pray such a manifest presence of the Lord that when saint or sinner walks over our threshold, they would inhale of Your savor.

Bring back loyalty, fidelity, trust, respect, compassion, gentleness, forbearance and covenant love. Give husbands and wives the grace to accept each other exactly the way they are, and not try to change each other, but to pray fervently one for another.

> "Bring back loyalty, fidelity, trust, respect, compassion, gentleness, forbearance and covenant love."

Just as You chose a wedding to perform Your first miracle of turning water into wine, so we ask You to breathe upon our homes and marriages, and turn that which has become mundane and bland into something pungent and powerful. Re-ignite our marriages, and let it be that when people observe them, they will get a glimpse of the Church for You said it's a mystery, but the Church is like marriage.

This morning we pray to restore fatherhood, that so important attribute from which the whole family in heaven and earth derives its name. Raise up the kind of fathers that when their sons observe them, they'll get a glimpse of their Heavenly Father, and want to spend time with Him.

Raise up the kind of mothers that daughters can emulate

and model and grow up to be fragrant handmaidens of the Lord.

Bring forth the kind of fathers and husbands that will be prophets and priests in their homes to represent God to their families and their families to God, and be a spiritual covering for their wives and children. We pray that husbands would so love and cherish their wives that they would find it easy to submit to them.

Just as You, Lord, were the Lamb of God and the Lion of Judah, we pray for men that will be so under the control of the Holy Spirit that they will know when to be like a gentle, tender lamb to their wives and children, and when to be transformed by Your Spirit into a valiant, militant, fierce lion against the enemy, and not get the two mixed up.

We pray for mothers and wives of noble character whose adornment is not external only, but whose main beauty is internal, women who are clothed with strength and dignity, whose children will rise up and call her blessed, and her husband will praise her.

We ask You, Lord, to bring children back from the land of captivity. Raise up a generation that will be so anointed that they will speak with the enemy at the gate. Let our sons be like olive plants around our table, and our daughters be like carved pillars to adorn a palace.

Blessed are the people of whom this is true. Blessed are the people whose God is the Lord.

In Jesus' name we pray, amen.

~24~

Prayer for Motherhood

Dear Lord, we pray that as this prayer broadcast goes out over Atlanta, that the anointing which accompanies with it would gently but powerfully penetrate the lives of the listeners and help them to realize that strength is available to lift them out of their tangled up, mired-down situation, that there is hope, that their circumstances have not gone too far for You to intervene. Come, Lord Jesus, be the lifter of the heads of Your people who are distraught by oppression and despair. Meet them exactly where they are, right now, and breathe upon them the breath of life. You are the Life-giver. Remove despair, hopelessness, depression. Replace it with joy unspeakable and full of glory, hope and a joyful expectation concerning the good things You are preparing to do for them in days to come. Lord, since You are so redemptive, we ask You to restore the years where the locust, cankerworm, palmer worm and caterpillar, all representative of evil malignant forces, restore the years where they have eaten.

Let them know by Your Spirit, it's not too late. The door is still open. Your grace is still extended. There is no sin too

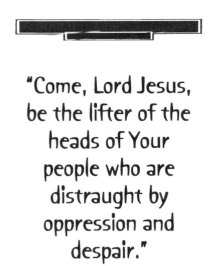

"Come, Lord Jesus, be the lifter of the heads of Your people who are distraught by oppression and despair."

great for Your blood to cleanse. Their lives haven't come to an end. As a matter of fact, we ask You, Lord, to etch into their minds and spirits that You have an incredible future for them which is full of hope and will not be cut off. What is being cut off as we speak, in the prayer of agreement, is everything the adversary has on his drawing boards. It will not come to pass. Destroy it now, in Jesus' name. We decree in the awesome, underestimated power of prayer agreement that only that which the Lord has intended for us from the foundations of this earth shall come to pass. Let Your people know this day You have destined them, You have called them. The calling is not only holy, but there is upon them a high and holy calling. Remind them, Lord, that they are the apple of Your eye, and they are members of a royal nation and a royal priesthood, and You are intently watching them this moment. You have not passed them by.

In preparation for Mother's Day this Sunday, we intercede for every mother listening to this prayer broadcast. Let them know one of the most vital and noble callings in all the world is to be a Godly mother. We pray right now to stand with them, encourage them, let there be released unto them wave after wave of the awesome presence of the Lord to affirm and confirm and reinforce and edify. Help them to know that the prayers they have prayed for loved ones, husbands and children have been heard and not to let up, but to tenaciously, relentlessly storm the gates of hell and knock on the gates of heaven until the answer comes. Give them grace to ask and keep on asking, seek and keep on seeking, knock and keep on knocking.

We pray for the elderly mothers, that instead of feeling like they're wasting away, getting weaker, that You quicken to them Your Word and the Divine process, as they trust You, that which is going on inside them right now, that though the outer man is perishing, the inner man is being renewed day by day. Quicken to them Your Word which states that as they trust You fully, they are going from one degree of grace to another, one degree of strength to another, and one degree of glory to another. Help them to know that Your retirement plan is to empower them in their golden years with resurrection energy as is stated in Psalm 71:18.

"Even when I am old and gray, do not forsake me, O God, till I declare your power to the next generation, your might to all who are to come."

We pray for their spiritual fortitude and strength, to take a resolute stand in prayer and we claim Your Word in Jeremiah 31:16, 17 when there was mourning and great weeping, Rachel weeping for her children and refusing to be comforted because her children were no more.

"This is what the Lord says: 'Restrain your voice from weeping and your eyes from tears, for your work will be rewarded,' declares the Lord. 'They will return from the land of the enemy.

So there is hope for your future,' declares the Lord, 'Your children will return to their own land.'"

Lord, we know there's nothing more powerful than praying Your Word back to You. We claim Your Scripture for those mothers who feel like their children are too hardened to sin, too deep into the world system, too anesthetized by the spirit of this age, too influenced by evil peer pressure, too deceived by the master of deception. Let this Scripture in Isaiah 49 be a rhema, quickened, pertinent Word to them right now which will cause them to be charged with supernatural encouragement concerning their children and their future.

"Can plunder be taken from warriors, or captives rescued from the fierce?

But this is what the Lord says: 'Yes, captives will be taken from warriors, and plunder retrieved from the fierce; I will contend with those who contend with you, and your children I will save.

I will make your oppressors eat their own flesh; they will be drunk on their own blood, as with wine. Then all mankind will know that I, the Lord, am your Savior, your Redeemer, the Mighty One of Jacob.'"

Isaiah 49:24-26

We pray for expectant mothers, that the child in their womb will be healthy and whole, without defects, perfectly formed, anointed like John the Baptist when he leaped in his mother Elizabeth's womb. Remove fear and panic, and the whisperings of the enemy. Let faith rise to a new level and let these little unborn ones be protected, come full term, and be part of the powerful generation You're raising up to dispossess the gates of the enemy and take back this land, little ones who are so anointed, as spoken of in Psalm 127:5, that they will contend and speak with the enemy at the gates. Let it be said of them as it says in Psalm 8:2,

"From the lips of children and infants you have ordained praise because of your enemies, to silence the foe and the avenger."

We pray that motherhood, which has been disdained and devalued by the feminist Jezebel influence in our society and taken a backseat to professional positions will once again be respected and venerated. Impress upon mothers all over this city that of all the work that's being accomplished out there, theirs is of the utmost importance. They are molding little lives. They are raising up future movers and shakers in the kingdom. They are leaving imprints on tiny minds. They are setting the course for future decision makers. They are discipling little apostles and prophets, pastors, teachers and evangelists. They are programming little minds in a Godly manner to be able to not only cope with a degenerate society, but to have the spiritual wherewithal to leave marks wherever they go. They are building character in little warriors and princesses not only to stand against the tide of a decadent generation, but to instill into them the backbone and moral fiber to take a resolute stand, be mouthpieces for the Lord, and to make a radical difference. Lord, we desperately need a young generation who will take a stand for godliness, righteousness and be counted.

In the midst of all of the mundane, routine chores of mothers, quicken to them that they are honored amongst women because You have chosen them to raise up a special generation which will be a vital part of this last day spiritual awakening and

"In the midst of all of the mundane, routine chores of mothers, quicken to them that they are honored amongst women. . . ."

probably witness the return of the Lord.

We pray for families where the mothers do not really have to work, but they have sacrificed their children in their formative years for more money, more material possessions and more prestige. Bring deep conviction to them and their husbands. Help them to make whatever lifestyle changes that are necessary and give them the resolve to make the decision that there is no more noble calling than a mother, and to concentrate on those things which have eternal value, and to make a priceless investment in their children.

For those mothers who have been forced into the marketplace to help make ends meet and there is no other way, give them grace, an extra measure of strength, and a heart of thanksgiving which will melt away any deep, low-grade resentment or bitterness which may rise up from time to time. Minister the kind of peace that passes all understanding that will melt away fear, agitation and fretfulness. Meet them, right now. Let there be a personal visitation from the Lord to encourage, reinforce and confirm, and give them the same anointing that the Proverbs 31 woman had to be industrious, frugal and, at the same time, the ability to smile at the future.

We pray that mothers all over this city will be greatly encouraged in the Lord. Give them Your mindset, Your perspective concerning their future. Be the lifter of their heads. Send them tokens for good. Bring such a wave of Your Spirit over them today that they would feel as if they have a new lease on life. We beseech You, Rapha Healer, the Great Physician, to touch their bodies. Let that same power that raised Christ Jesus from the dead, resurrection power, flow profusely through their bodies. Reinvigorate, refurbish, renew, resuscitate. Be their oxygen line. We claim what You did on the cross for them. Banish pain, sickness and disease from their bodies. We claim Psalm 103. You forgive all of our iniquities. You heal all of our diseases. Thank You, Lord, for being gracious to our mothers. They have left an incredible legacy to us.

In Jesus' name, amen.

~25~

Prayer for
the Christmas Season

During this Christmas season, we thank You, Lord, that You humbled Yourself and came into this world in the form of a little baby. We acknowledge You as our Redeemer, Savior, Baptizer, Healer, Lord and Master. We have no other master. More than ever before, as we are on the threshold of a very significant year, be the Lord of our lives.

We pray this would be the most momentous and significant Christmas season that those listening would ever experience. We pray that family gatherings would not just be social, but that they would be so saturated in prayer that the presence of the Lord would come in like a sweet fragrance and nobody would leave there the same. We pray that this Christmas, we would not be caught up in the hectic, frenzied pace of commercialism, but our hearts would be gripped by You, that we would be strangely warmed, and find ourselves being drawn into communion with You and Your Word. We present ourselves afresh and anew to You this morning. Captivate us. Draw us to Yourself. Let us describe ourselves as Paul did— love slaves of Jesus Christ. Let it be that we are totally intrigued and enamored by You. At the culmination of this

"At the culmination
of this year, and on
the threshold of a
brand new year,
give us a passion
for Jesus."

year, and on the threshold of a brand new year, give us a passion for Jesus. Let the zeal of the Lord of hosts consume us and let that be the only consumption we ever experience. What better gift for ourselves and others in this new year than to bring us from religion to relationship.

Lord, in the midst of man's government, which oftentimes becomes corrupt and tainted, we thank You for Your government which has no end to the increase of its peace. We invite the Prince of Peace, the Lord Jesus Christ, to rule and reign over our lives with peace this day. Let there be the rustling of Your garments in every room of our homes. Remove anxiety, fear, and tension and stress. In Jesus' name, take away nervousness, pressure, panic, pain. Restore to us Your tranquility. Right now, especially during the accelerated pace of shopping and last minute holiday preparations and everyday cares and duties, we cast our heavy burdens upon You. Thank You, Lord, You are our burden bearer.

We pray Your Word that You will keep in perfect peace that person whose mind is steadfast and stays on You because they trust in You. We speak the peace of the Lord to descend upon Atlanta, the peace which is indescribable, nor can be articulated. There are no superlatives to define it. It's the peace that passes all understanding.

Lord, right now, we pray this Word back to You.

"Peace I leave with you; my peace I give you. I do not give to you as the world gives. Do not let your hearts be troubled and do not be afraid."

John 14:27

We thank You, Lord, that You have something beyond any drugs, medication or therapy this world has to offer. In the world there is the law of diminishing returns. Whatever it offers, there must be more and more to provide the same results. The results are diminishing and they are only superficial. They're artificial, just for a fleeting moment. Thank You, Lord, that Your peace is just the opposite. Instead of decreasing, it increases. There is more and more. Lord, bring an increase of peace in the lives of those listening today. Indeed, You will keep them in perfect peace him whose mind is steadfast because he trusts in You (Isaiah 26:3).

Thank You, Lord, that this Christmas season, all who are weary and burdened can come to You and You will give them rest. We take Your yoke upon us to learn of You, knowing You are gentle and humble in heart and we find rest for our souls. Your yoke is easy. Your burden is light.

We thank You for Your Word which states in Isaiah 32:17 and 18,

"The fruit of righteousness will be peace; the effect of righteousness will be quietness and confidence forever.

My people will live in peaceful dwelling places, in secure homes, in undisturbed places of rest."

Let Your peace flow like a river, Your righteousness like

waves of the sea. We are eternally grateful to You, Lord. You paid the ultimate price. You were pierced for our transgressions, crushed for our iniquities. The punishment that brought us peace was upon You and by Your wounds we are healed.

We ask You, Lord, this Christmas season, to descend upon us like a cloud of glory. Let Your manifest presence accompany us wherever we go. Let this be one of the richest fellowship times with You and others we have ever known. Break down walls, burst through impasses, crush the evil opposition, lift off heavy foreboding clouds of oppression, bring healing virtue in an unprecedented manner, comfort the mourning, bind up the wounds, deliver answers to prayers. This Christmas, let there be expressions of Your character in our lives. Let Your people flourish in the courts of the Lord, in the land of the living. Give them a new lease on life and let this be the preparation time for a brand new year—so different, so full of light, so loaded with promise that it will not be worthy to be compared to last year.

We thank You this morning, Lord, that You are our Wonderful Counselor—wonderful in counsel and magnificent in wisdom. You are the One Who leads the blind by ways they have not known, along unfamiliar paths. You turn darkness into light and make rough places smooth. We ask You to guide us always.

Thank You for sending the Holy Spirit, another counselor, the Spirit of Truth. We pray that those listening would not only be baptized in Your Holy Spirit, but be inundated by the power of God. Remove them from a rut. Lead them out of a bland, mundane existence, out of sterile, impotent religion, out of just hanging on and being a survivor, out of a place of mediocrity and bring them across the river, out of a land, laboring under a cruel taskmaster, making bricks without straw, in a city tightly shut up, in a narrow pass and be a strong deliverer. Bring them across the river to a Promised Land that spontaneously flows with milk and honey and water springs out of every valley and mountain. Where the Spirit of the Lord is, there is liberty. Let Your people know, by experience, firsthand, what it means that in Your presence is fullness of joy and at Your right hand are pleasures forevermore.

> **"Let Your people know, by experience, firsthand, what it means that in Your presence is fullness of joy. . . ."**

For those of Your children who are in the valley of decision and must have answers real soon, we pray that they, at this crucial moment, would not receive just human, fleshly, intellectual counsel or advice, or just go by the seeing of their eyes or the hearing of their ears, but that You would burst on the scene with a rhema word, the Word of the Lord for this critical situation—a fresh, inspired, anointed Word that would be quickened and confirmed unto them and they would know that they know that they know.

Lord, You are not only our Wonderful Counselor, but we celebrate You this day as our Mighty God. We receive the impartation of Your nature which sustains us. As Isaiah 58 says, satisfy our needs in a sun-scorched land and strengthen our frame. Dispel the weakness, the exhaustion, the fatigue, the dissipation of energies. Put to flight the evil one who robs Your people of their strength and impart resurrection power, the very same power that raised Christ Jesus from the grave. Let it flow into our being. Help us to experience what it says in Isaiah 40:31 (KJV), *". . .They that wait upon the Lord shall renew their strength; they shall mount up with wings as eagles; they shall run and not be weary; . . .they shall walk, and not faint."*

We speak Your Word to Your servants this day. As is stated in Psalm 18, arm us with strength for the battle. Cause our adversaries to bow at our feet. Psalm 21:13, *". . .in your strength; we will sing and praise your might."* Psalm 28, You Lord, are our strength and shield, our heart trusts in You. We are helped. Our heart leaps for joy. You are our refuge and strength, an ever present help in trouble. We will sing of Your strength in the morning. Summon Your power, O God. Show us Your strength. Let this be different from any other Christmas season. At the height of it, let us enter into Your season of refreshing and drink at Your fountain this day.

Lord, You are not only our Wonderful Counselor and Mighty God, but we celebrate You this morning as our Everlasting Father. We ask You to be a loving Father to those who have none, to those who have had absentee fathers. We pray fatherhood to be restored to Your Church. Send the spirit of Elijah, the great intercessor, to turn the hearts of the fathers to the children and the hearts of the children to the fathers so the curse of rejection can be lifted off our land. For those who are feeling rejected, let them realize that regardless of what has transpired in the past, that You bore the curse of rejection on the cross and they are accepted in the Beloved.

We celebrate You, Lord, as the Incarnate Word, that the Word became flesh and dwelt among us. In the beginning was the Word and the Word was with God, and the Word was

God. We acknowledge this morning, that in Scripture, one of Your names is, the Word of God. Thank You, Lord Jesus, that You, the Word became flesh, above the raucous noise and frenzied, hectic turmoil of the season, let this be real to us—the Word became flesh.

We pray for a revival of the Word in Atlanta, that the incarnate Word, which is the reason we celebrate Christmas, would become incarnate in us. Let the Logos, the written Word, be so breathed upon by Your Spirit, that it gently explodes in our lives into rhema—the inspired, anointed Word. Bring a revival of the Word in our personal lives. Let it be ignited and anointed by Your Holy Spirit. Let us be intrigued and enamored by Your Word. We thank You that when the Word comes alive to use, we never get bored. As Paul said, it is unsearchable. There's always more.

Forever, O Lord, Your Word is settled in heaven. It is immutable. It is unchangeable. It is infallible. It is inspired. We cannot thank You enough for the first Christmas when You, the Word, the Lord Jesus Christ, humbled Yourself, to come in the form of a little baby, to be the Savior of the world. We realize one of the most powerful personal experiences is praying Your Word back to You. Raise up intercessors, powerful prayer warriors, who know how to stand in the gap, make up the hedge, weep between the altar and the porch, take an assignment all the way to the gates, and won't rest nor give You rest until the glory of the Lord shines through into our personal lives, into the Church, and into this nation. Lord, bring Your glory back into Your Church.

In Jesus' name, amen.

Additional Scripture Reference

Isaiah 9:2-7

The people walking in darkness have seen a great light; on those living in the land of the shadow of death a light has dawned. You have enlarged the nation and increased their joy; they rejoice before you as people rejoice at the harvest, as men rejoice when dividing the plunder. For as in the day of Midian's defeat, you have shattered the yoke that burdens them, the bar across their shoulders, the rod of their oppressor. Every warrior's boot used in battle and every garment rolled in blood will be destined for burning, will be fuel for the fire. For to us a child is born, to us a son is given, and the government will be on his shoulders. And he will be called Wonderful Counselor, Mighty God, Everlasting Father, Prince of Peace. Of the increase of his government and peace there will be no end. He will reign on David's throne and over his kingdom, establishing and upholding it with justice and righteousness from that time on and forever. The zeal of the Lord Almighty will accomplish this.

~26~

Prayer for
the New Year

Dear Lord, we thank You that Your compassions never fail. They are new every morning. You daily load us with benefits and great is Your faithfulness. We pray that this year will be one of awakening. Let it be different. We appropriate Your Word in Isaiah 64:1-5 for the days ahead.

"Oh, that you would rend the heavens and come down, that the mountains would tremble before you!

As when fire sets twigs ablaze and causes water to boil, come down to make your name known to your enemies and cause the nations to quake before you!

. . .you did awesome things that we did not expect, ...

Since ancient times no one has heard, no ear has perceived, no eye has seen any God besides you, who acts on behalf of those who wait for him.

You come to the help of those who gladly do right, . . ."

We also thank You for Your Word in First Corinthians 2:9, 10.

". . .no eye has seen, no ear has heard, no mind has conceived what God has prepared for those who love him—

but God has revealed it to us by his Spirit. . . ."

We repent for having made peace with mediocrity, for lapsing into a slough of despondency and self-pity, for allowing life to become routine and stale, and for falling into a rut. By the grace of God, it's going to be different.

We ask You, Lord, to re-program our mind. Give us Your mindset, the mind of Christ. Impart to us Your perspective, Your outlook on the future. Pull the curtain back. Give us Your vision and give us an expectancy of Your miracle-working power in our lives.

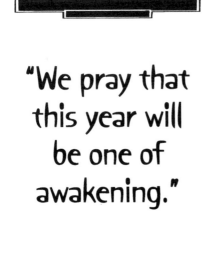

"We pray that this year will be one of awakening."

We invite You to come. Upset the status quo. Let it not be business as usual in our lives nor in the Church. Remove the impasses, break through stalemates, crush the resistance, tear down opposition. We pray that walls the enemy has built to frustrate, exasperate and vex us, this morning would crash and burn. Give us the grace to speak to mountains and pray powerful, effectual, fervent prayers that avail much and see angels dispatched to facilitate Your purposes. You're the God of breakthroughs, the God of the impossible, the God of new beginnings.

We thank You, Lord, that You specialize in swinging into action once we have expended all of our resources, run out of all options, and drained our brilliant, fleshly humanistic think tanks. We, once again, celebrate You this morning and honor You as an above and beyond God, One Who is well able to do exceedingly abundantly above all that we can ask or think. Come, Lord Jesus, on the threshold of a brand new year. Show yourself powerful to Your people, reveal Your right arm, press these battles to the gates, and get glory to Yourself.

This morning, we ask You to strike supernatural hope and encouragement into the heart of Your saints. Lift them out of their shriveled-up view of the future. Give them Your outlook, Your attitude and Your perspective. Let them smell the smoke of victory in the camp. Impart to them Godly gusto. Whatever is going on in the heavenlies because of their faithful prayers over a long period of time, let that great reservoir in heaven which contains prayers mixed with incense suddenly come cascading down onto earth in some tangible, concrete form, in the form of healing or finances or reconciliation of relationships, or the salvation of a lost loved one. Be the lifter of their heads and give them such a spirit of conquest, like Joshua, in his latter years, that all he would have to do is look at a mountain, seeing an opportunity, and say, "I'll take it. Give me that mountain." Give them such a mindset of conquest, that they will say as Daniel said in chapter 11, verse 32 that the people that know their God shall be strong, and do exploits. Let this year go down in their personal history as an unprecedented year of great exploits.

We praise You for Your Word in Jeremiah 29:11-13.

"'For I know the plans I have for you,' declares the Lord, 'plans to prosper you and not to harm you, plans to give you hope and a future.

Then you will call upon me and come and pray to me, and I will listen to you.

You will seek me and find me when you seek me with all your heart.'"

We believe with all of our heart that the best yet lies ahead, that You are a God of increase, that You are taking us from one degree of glory to another, one degree of grace to another, and from strength to strength, and that our future is as bright as the promises of God. You are the God of the new beginning. What better time to experience this than right now. Remove all hindrances to what You are about to do in our lives.

Every time we hear bad news on NBC, ABC, or CNN, we are greatly encouraged in the Lord because as Your Word states in Isaiah 60, even though darkness covers the earth and gross darkness the people, in direct proportion, the light of the Lord is arising upon us and Your awesome glory is appearing over Your Church. As a matter of fact, the light will be so bright that nations and kings will come just to check it out.

This year we don't want to just be in an existence mode or just have a survival mentality. We want to experience what You meant when You said that You not only bring life, but bring it more abundantly. We want to draw deeply from the wells of salvation. Let it be that out of our innermost being will flow rivers of living water, and we say to this reservoir, "Spring up, O well."

In the name of Jesus, amen.

Additional Scripture References

Isaiah 44:3
For I will pour water on the thirsty land, and streams on the dry ground; I will pour out my Spirit on your offspring, and my blessing on your descendants.

Isaiah 42:9, 10
See, the former things have taken place, and new things I declare; before they spring into being I announce them to you. Sing to the Lord a new song, his praise from the ends of the earth. . . .

Isaiah 35:1-4
The desert and the parched land will be glad; the wilderness will rejoice and blossom. Like the crocus, it will burst into bloom; . . .they will see the glory of the Lord, the splendor of our God. Strengthen the feeble hands, steady the knees that give way; say to those with fearful hearts, "Be strong, do not fear; your God will come, he will come with vengeance; with divine retribution he will come to save you."

Isaiah 43:18-21
Forget the former things; do not dwell on the past. See, I am doing a new thing! Now it springs up; do you not perceive it? I am making a

way in the desert and streams in the wasteland. . . .I provide water in the desert and streams in the wasteland, to give drink to my people, my chosen, the people I formed for myself that they proclaim my praise.

Philippians 3:13, 14
. . .one thing I do: Forgetting what is behind and straining toward what is ahead, I press on toward the goal to win the prize for which God has called me heavenward in Christ Jesus.

DAVID L. THOMAS
(1939-2000)

David L. Thomas was an ordained minister and co-founder of *Intercessors International, Inc.* With over 30 years in ministry, he served in many capacities, some of which were—interim pastor, missionary, corporate and hospital chaplain, television and radio speaker, board member of several ministries, guest speaker at churches, conferences and seminars around the country, and on numerous occasions, led the National Day of Prayer from the square in Marietta, GA as well as from the capitol steps in Atlanta, GA. Prayer was his belief and passion with a strong desire to see the House of God turned back into a House of Prayer for all nations.

INTERCESSORS INTERNATIONAL, INC.

P. O. Box 450093
Atlanta, GA 31145
(404) 330-1906

Intercessors International, Inc. is a 501(c)(3), non-profit ministry founded by David and Lynn Thomas as an international, non-denominational, full gospel intercessory prayer ministry to network, instruct, challenge, encourage and call forth intercessors in preparation for the last day harvest and spiritual awakening. One of their primary burdens is to see the modern American Church reduced back to the simplicity which is in Christ Jesus (2 Corinthians 11:3), and returned back to its initial mandate to be known as a House of Prayer for all nations (Mark 11:17). This is accomplished by a "Jeremiah Prayer Anointing" which uproots, tears down, destroys and overthrows man's humanistic religion so the Lord can build and plant His true New Testament Church (Jeremiah 1:10). They strongly believe in Paul's admonition, "the kingdom of God is not a matter of talk, but of power" (1 Corinthians 4:20).

THE POWER OF
"DECIMAL, DECIMATING"
PRAYER

5-3/8 x 8-1/4   112 pages
Quality Paperback
ISBN# 0-9718249-3-2

This book details the power and importance of corporate prayer.
When believers come together to pray, their prayers have the potential
to change any situation, no matter how big or how small. Titles
include:

♦ *One of Satan's Main Tactics*
♦ *The Amazing Power of Just One Person's Prayers*
♦ *Why You Have Been So Resisted*
♦ *Prayer Exposes the Enemy*

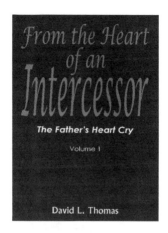

FROM THE HEART OF AN INTERCESSOR
VOLUME 1
The Father's Heart Cry
5-3/8 x 8-1/4   144 pages
Quality Paperback
ISBN# 0-9718249-1-6

This book contains a collection of intercessory prayers for our nation and churches, as well as individual issues in our lives. We are the last great prayer generation. In David L. Thomas' own words:

"This is not just any generation. There is a portion of the remnant who have heard from God, consider it a critical mandate which at all costs must be carried out, do not want to compromise, and have opted to take the high road. These are people who have set their faces like flint, burned their bridges behind them, launched into the deep, put their hands to the plow and are not about to look back."

To order additional copies of:

- *From The Heart of an Intercessor Volume 2*
- *The Power of "Decimal, Decimating" Prayer,*
  or
- *From The Heart of an Intercessor Volume 1*, contact:

Anderson Publishing
P. O. Box 5544
Douglasville, GA 30154

e-mail address:
canderson@andersonpub.com

website address:
www.andersonpub.com